The Seven Deadly Sins

The Seven Deadly Sins

and how to overcome them

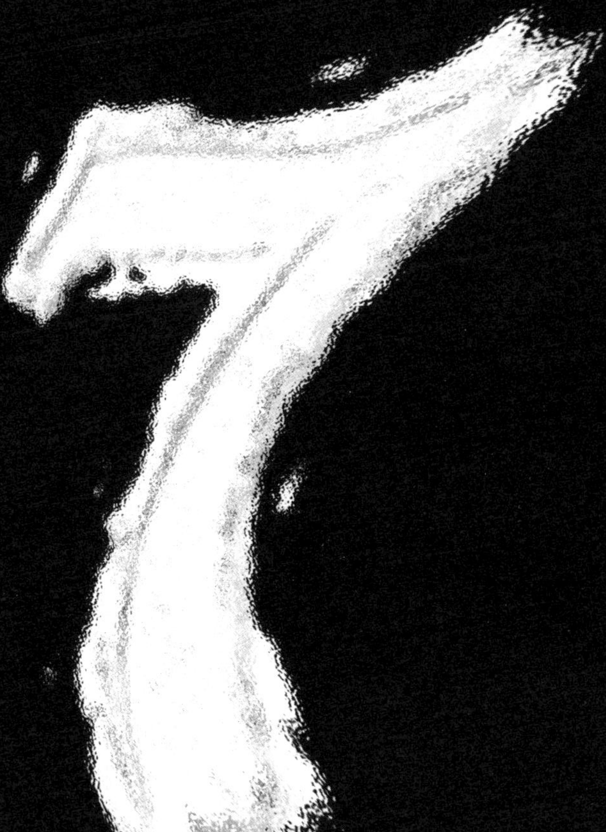

Graham Tomlin

A Lion Book
an imprint of
Lion Hudson plc
Wilkinson House, Jordan Hill Road,
Oxford OX2 8DR, England
www.lionhudson.com
ISBN 978 0 7459 5221 5
ISBN 978 0 8254 6258 0

First edition 2007
10 9 8 7 6 5 4 3 2 1

Text Acknowledgments

p. 8 'It's a Sin' lyrics by Neil Tennant/Christopher Lowe
© Sony/ATV Music Publishing. All Rights Reserved.
pp. 9, 30, 37, 67, 65, 71, 75–76, 77, 79, 90, 93, 94, 99, 105, 109, 126, 138 Scripture quotations taken from the Holy Bible, New International Version, copyright © 1973, 1978, 1984 International Bible Society. Used by permission of Zondervan and Hodder & Stoughton Limited. All rights reserved. The 'NIV' and 'New International Version' trademarks are registered in the United States Patent and Trademark Office by International Bible Society. Use of either trademark requires the permission of International Bible Society. UK trademark number 1448790.

Picture Acknowledgments

p. 7 Don Smith/Alamy
p. 33 Mediacolor's/Alamy
p. 55 CoverSpot/Alamy
p. 81 Darren Robb/Alamy
p. 101 UNIVERSAL/CELANDINE/MONTY PYTHON/THE KOBAL COLLECTION
p. 121 SUNNYphotography.com/Alamy
p. 143 David Hoffman Photo Library/Alamy
p. 163 Chad Ehlers/Alamy

This book has been printed on paper and board independently certified as having been produced from sustainable forests.

A catalogue record for this book is available
from the British Library

Typeset in 12/16pt Egyptian 505
Printed and bound by Gutenberg Press

Distributed by:
UK: Marston Book Services Ltd, PO Box 269, Abingdon, Oxon OX14 4YN
USA: Trafalgar Square Publishing, 814 N Franklin Street, Chicago, IL 60610
USA Christian Market: Kregel Publications, PO Box 2607, Grand Rapids, Michigan 49501

Contents

Acknowledgments

Writing a book requires a good deal of work, and not just from one person. Several friends read chapters and gave invaluable advice, did background research and contributed in different ways to the creation of this one. Thanks are due especially to Sally Harding, Nicky and Sila Lee, Rebekah Lummis, Hector and Caroline Sants, Graham Singh, Tim Sudworth, Ruth Walley, and Stu and Susie Wright for their different contributions. Morag Reeve and the team at Lion Hudson were their usual encouraging, efficient and helpful selves. Strangely all my friends seemed rather reluctant to have a book on the seven deadly sins dedicated to them, so I've not done anyone the disservice of that dubious honour. As always, my greatest debt remains to Janet, from whom I learn every day about virtue and kindness, and Sam and Siân, who together mean the world to me.

1 Sins and the Soul

The word 'sin' has a chequered past. *Peccato, péché, Sünde,* sin; whatever language it came in, it was once a terrifying word – a word that struck fear into the heart of almost every European. It had the same kind of emotional effect as words such as 'Nazi' or 'cancer' do for us today. It was something they wanted to avoid at all costs, something dreadful and dangerous.

Now, it has changed from a rottweiler into a poodle. 'Sin' has been calmed down, domesticated, neutered. The word is now usually spoken with a slight smirk, or a heavy dose of irony. Describing something as 'sinful' usually means we think it is naughty but nice, in the spirit of 'I know I shouldn't really, but it will be fun, and I'm sure it won't do any harm.' At other times, 'sinful' describes something proscribed by people who just want to stop other people from enjoying themselves. The Pet Shop Boys' song 'It's a Sin' carries the tone of the oppressed victim, told by finger-wagging killjoys in authority that whatever he does or desires is wrong:

When I look back upon my life
It's always with a sense of shame
I've always been the one to blame
For everything I long to do
No matter when or where or who
Has one thing in common, too:

It's a sin
Everything I've ever done
Everything I ever do
Every place I've ever been
Everywhere I'm going to
It's a sin

Given all the negativity of the past, it's not surprising that we want to draw the sting out of such an unpleasant idea, defuse the word, emasculate it, draw out its old venom.

Yet there was a very simple reason why the word 'sin' had such a ghastly aura about it in the past. Sin was not harmless transgression of some random moral code invented by repressed and frustrated medieval clerics. For our ancestors, 'sin' described a pattern of life that was quite simply destructive. It destroyed families, friendships, happiness, peace of mind, innocence, love, security, nature and, most importantly, our bond to our creator. It wrenched us out of our proper place in the world. It put the world out of joint, skewing everything and spreading misery and pain everywhere. A passage in the Bible talks of 'sinful desires, which war against your soul' (1 Peter 2:11). That captures it well: these impulses, these patterns of behaviour were not just arbitrarily wrong, but were quite literally self-destructive. They waged a constant, subtle and undermining warfare against the inner self; they were the deadly enemy of the soul. What seemed on the surface to be innocent pleasures, or even the promise of an experience that made life worth living, in reality slowly tore people apart. Sin was a like a virus that got into everything, so that although life carried on, it never quite worked in the way we felt it ought to. Life always had that grit in the corner of the eye; the nagging soreness of a shoe that doesn't fit; the reminder of a dark secret that won't go away.

So this book is an attempt at rehabilitation, or perhaps 'dehabilitation': restoring 'sin' to its proper place, sending it back to the pit where it belongs. It is a journey through the dark lowlands of sin to the bright landscapes of goodness.

Breaking the Rules or Destroying the Soul?

Why has our understanding of sin undergone such a change? Why do we not fear it as much as we did? Perhaps it is because we have allowed a lop-sided view of it to take hold. In many people's minds, 'sin' means simply 'breaking the rules'. If that's all it is, the question that arises (especially for a generation conditioned by every possible method of educational philosophy to ask questions) is: 'Whose rules?' We might reply, 'God's rules', but that doesn't make it any better. Who is to say what God's rules are? Who interprets God's commands for us and tells us what they should be? Of course the reply to this question used to be 'the church', but then we're back with our original problem. Can we really trust the church to tell us what to do, this fallible body of (mostly) aging men, whose own moral record is hardly spotless?

The difficulty is that the conception of sin as 'breaking the rules' does not go to the heart of it. A fixation with 'keeping the rules' for their own sake usually betrays that someone has got it wrong somewhere, and not surprisingly – and with some justification – we feel a glimmer of rebellion stirring within us. An insistence on law alone is often a sign of a shrivelled, arid moral vision. It's what makes disapproving busybodies and prudes. Laws exist to protect things that are more important than laws. They are not ends in themselves. When we understand that laws are protective, there to guard vital and valuable things such as human lives, families, marriages, reputations, communities and peace, then we begin to understand their true function. Laws are vital for the protection of goodness, but they do not themselves go to the heart of goodness; they simply try to ensure its survival.

So it is perhaps best to see sin, or sins, not so much as breaking the rules, but rather as destructive habits. This book sees the seven deadly sins as 'seven habits of highly destructive people'. They are patterns of life which, if we let them take control of us, will unravel all that is good in our lives, and will lead us to destroy everything around us. That is why they are to be avoided. However, there is one particular thing about sin that goes to the heart of why Christian moral teaching has always seen it in such stark terms.

Life Together

There is a story of a Scottish woman who came back from her Presbyterian church one morning to her unbelieving husband who had stayed at home. He asked her what the sermon was about. 'The minister preached about sin,' she said. 'What did he say about it?' replied her husband. The answer came back: 'He was against it.'

Why do Christians fuss about sin? Why spoil a little harmless fun with such a negative and doleful outlook on life? The answer is important and often misunderstood, and in one way can be stated quite simply: life is meant to be lived together, but sin isolates us.

The Christian God is not a simple, solitary figure, the lonely old man with the beard and flowing robes beloved of cartoonists everywhere. Instead, he is, as the theologians put it, 'three in one'. Without going into the fine details of such theological mathematics, it simply means that God, as Christians understand him, is neither plural nor unitary. The ancient pagans, whether Greek or barbarian, thought there were lots of different gods. The often unstated implication lurking behind this view of the world was a belief that ultimate reality was also plural: irredeemably varied and disparate. The problem with this is that it is hard to find any underlying unity or deep-seated reason to expect things to hold together. The nagging fear is that if underlying reality is varied and plural, then life ultimately is based on conflict between irreconcilable powers or perspectives, and there is no way of ever resolving them.

On the other hand, traditional monotheism held that there was just one single, uncomplicated God. This has the advantage of being easy to understand and gets over the difficulty of polytheism: the anxiety that all there ultimately is is endless, irresolvable divergence. But – and it is a big 'but', especially in the modern world – monotheism carries with it the deep fear that everything has to fit in with this one, simple God, and that we all have to be dragooned into line in a dreary, boring sameness. For many modern people, monotheism threatens difference and therefore also threatens art, creativity, variety and liberty; and perhaps they have a point. And sometimes monotheists are so convinced that everyone needs to be brought into line that they are willing to resort to violence to impose it. A belief that ultimate reality is unitary, simple and monochrome threatens us with the possibility that we will all be made to follow suit. Polytheism threatens to bring chaos, monotheism threatens to bring coercion. Polytheism offers too much freedom, monotheism offers too little.

In the light of their experience of God being present with them in the person of Jesus and in the mysterious experience of the Holy Spirit, the early Christians worked out an understanding of God that was consciously different from either of these. Unlike the Greek and Roman paganism and the Jewish monotheism that surrounded them, the God of the Christians was 'three in one' – made up of Father, Son and Holy Spirit. However, this didn't add up to three gods; the three were somehow bound together in a fundamental unity of mutual love. If this was true of God, then it was also true of the world. The result was a view of life that held together the ultimate unity of all things *and* the beauty of variety and difference.

If true, this of course means that these two major human fears – that on the one hand, nothing lies at the end of the rainbow but irreconcilable perspectives and unceasing discord, and that on the other, all we find there is dull uniformity – begin to evaporate. Instead, ultimate reality, God himself, is unity in variety. Difference is to be celebrated, yet not limitless difference. Difference is ultimately held together by love and self-giving. It is a view of the world that values differences of race, personality, taste, gender and gifts, and yet sees them all blend together in a harmony of delight and tunefulness.

There is another important step in this argument. For Christians, humans are said to be made 'in the image of God'. In other words, we are made in some way to resemble God, to reflect something of his nature and to care for the world in his name. If that is true, we might expect something of this same 'unity in difference' to be true of us as well. Over the past couple of hundred years, especially in Western societies, we have tended to think of ourselves primarily as individuals, free to make our own independent choices. We might occasionally choose to associate with other people whom we happen to like, but at root we are independent of each other, free in our sovereign rights over our own bodies and souls. The Christian faith sees it differently. Our true nature is not found in individuality but in belonging. We find our true identity in relationship to others, not in isolation from them; in interdependence, not independence. We are first and foremost members of families, neighbourhoods, societies and friendships before we are individuals. Of course we are individuals and we do have an important measure of personal freedom, but just as God is diversity in unity, so too are we. As the book of Genesis suggests, it is not good for us to be alone.

When Jesus spoke about the goal of human life, he often used an illustration common in the Old Testament: a vision of a huge banquet, tables laden with colourful, succulent food and rich red wine, all tucked into by a noisy, warm and intimate group of friends, with lots of laughter, delight and satisfaction. It's not the kind of picture we normally associate with religion, but then again, Jesus rarely seemed to fit the expectations of religious people. The point of it is that this is where human life is heading. This is how it is meant to be lived: in harmony, fellowship and with grace.

Sometimes we go to a party where, despite apparent bonhomie, under the surface there is an undercurrent of jealousy, subtle competition as to who can tell the best jokes or impress the most by their jobs, income or achievements, or barely concealed antagonism and friction. The best parties take place among friends, where none of this rears its head. We can imagine an evening spent with our best friends, where no-one feels the need to impress, everyone is out to ensure that everyone else has the best of times, and all we experience is the generosity of a good host, the kindness of good people and the sheer fun of being with those we love and who love us. That is the picture we get in the Bible of the true goal of human life. It is meant to be lived together, with everyone included.

What does this all have to do with sin? Goodness enables us to live well together; to let our differences from each other blend into something creative, beautiful and enjoyable. Sin, on the other hand, destroys this harmony and ensures that our differences lead to misery and pain. The very things that destroy a good evening together – things like envy, pride, lust or anger – are what is described as sin. As we shall see, anger, jealousy and pride break friendships, destroy communities and leave people in solitary, lonely isolation. Of course, solitude is not a bad thing; we need it from time to time to restore perspectives and to reorient ourselves. Yet it is not ultimately what we are made for. We are made for fellowship, for friendship, to be together with others. And sin, in the Christian view of the world, is whatever renders us incapable of doing that and breaks our bonds to each other and ultimately to God, who gives life and breath and joy.

Sin isolates us. It makes us unable to maintain a healthy relationship with anyone. I remember travelling through India some years ago, and meeting an aged hippy who had somehow got left behind from the 1960s and grown old on drugs, travelling and Indian religion. It was hard to work out what was cause and what was effect, but the result of twenty years' travelling on his own had created a thoroughly neurotic, angular and tortured soul. He had hardly maintained a relationship for longer than a week for the past ten years and distrusted everyone. He was a bundle of nerves, suspecting everyone of trying to rip him off and full of jealousy, rage and tension. Encountering him was like meeting a hissing cobra: the nearer I got, the more dangerous he seemed. When I met him, he had been beaten up, robbed of the little he'd owned and left for dead in a filthy gutter. A group of Christian friends of mine had taken him in and begun to look after him, and slowly he had started to unwind and learn to relate to people again. It was a salutary lesson in what destructive behaviour can do. It isolates us, turns everyone into a real or potential enemy and ultimately makes life a living hell. It was also a lesson in finding the way back – the path of grace and virtue.

So it is vital, if we are to live good, healthy lives, enjoying good, healthy relationships, that we learn to avoid those patterns of behaviour that destroy us and the people we love, and in turn learn the habits of life that build strong lives and communities. In other words, it's vital that we learn as far as we can to find a way to stop 'doing sin'.

Sin and Seduction

The complication for us is that contemporary culture in the West has not only rehabilitated the word 'sin'; it has also rehabilitated almost all of the individual sins, so that far from being ugly, repulsive terrors, they have become subtly and enticingly attractive to us. Lust, envy and greed sell newspapers, cars and exotic foodstuffs, so naturally there are powerful forces dedicated to encouraging these habits to grow as rampantly as possible in our souls and societies.

Yet it's not just our contemporary world that has discovered the delights of sin. Our forebears were not as innocent as we might think. Of course they didn't *all* detest sin, because it has always carried a very real and powerful attraction. And unless we grasp this we will never understand it. Life would be simple if things that were bad for us were ugly and things that were good for us were beautiful. But life isn't like that. As the great Augustine said of his own younger tendency towards theft just for the sake of it: 'It was foul, and I loved it.' As we look at each sin in turn, we'll see how subtly seductive they have become for us.

The great works that have dealt with sin in the past had a simple aim: to uncover the ugliness of sin and unmask the veneer of attractiveness that it wears. Dante's *Divine Comedy*, one of the greatest works of European literature, did this in the thirteenth century by showing what these patterns of behaviour led to. It showed how each received its fitting punishment in a vision of such elegant symmetry that it seems obvious. In Dante's imaginary hell, the angry are condemned to fight each other for eternity; the gluttonous are made to lie in mud, exposed to constant rain and hail just like the pigs their behaviour copied, and end up eating rats, toads and snakes as a parody of their excessive greed; the slothful or indolent are condemned to running constantly and breathlessly, and so on.

Yet strangely, each sin always has at its heart something good. Medieval artistic depictions of sins portrayed them as misshapen and deformed versions of some good quality. The reason is not hard to find. Lust takes the delights to be found in sexual desire and satisfaction and distorts it into an uncontrollable, damaging enslavement. Gluttony twists the pleasures of succulent roast beef and a glass of dark red Beaujolais and turns them into bloated, sickly over-consumption.

There is always something of the grotesque about sin. In old fairgrounds, there was usually one stall where you could place yourself in front of oddly shaped mirrors, which would exaggerate some parts of your body and shrink others. The result was funny but at the same time slightly frightening. Sin does the same thing. It takes something beautiful and makes it ugly by twisting it out of shape so that it bears enough resemblance to the original to retain its attraction, but when seen in its full light it is as ugly as… well, sin. On one level, it is funny. Most of our jokes revolve around the grotesque: things out of place, misshapen, strange. Yet there is a dark side as well and it is this that these medieval imaginative poems tried to unveil. The theologian Cornelius Plantinga says: 'A sinful life is a partly depressing, partly ludicrous caricature of genuine human life.'

This takes us on to something very important about the nature of sin and evil. Although it can seem a monstrous and terrifying power that threatens to overwhelm everything, in the end evil can only ever distort something that is essentially good. Evil cannot create anything; it simply twists, caricatures or destroys. Sin is always a parody, a type of behaviour that often looks vaguely like goodness and often likes to pretend it is, and it usually takes some moral and spiritual discernment to tell the difference. Yet a difference there surely is, and the ability to tell good from evil is a real sign of human and personal maturity. But the reason why it is often difficult to tell which is which is that sin always has at its heart something good. It always takes something precious or valuable and mangles it, distorts it and makes it ugly, turning a swan into an ugly duckling. When we experience a fit of temper against a brother, sister or child, we usually justify ourselves with the behaviour that provoked their anger in the first place, which probably was out of order. Jealousy and envy persuade us that they are really proper outrage against a deep injustice that has given to someone else what we deserve.

This means of course that however monstrous sin and evil are, in the Christian view of the world, they are ultimately trivial and pathetic when compared with real goodness. Augustine struggled all his life to understand the nature of malevolence. Towards the end of his life, the reality of evil began to recede from his attention, to be replaced by something much bigger. As the Cambridge historian Gillian Evans puts it: 'Where first he had been aware of [evil's] perverseness and emptiness, its huge darkness, its hopeless entangled knottiness, now at last perhaps he had come to feel its essential triviality in comparison with the light and power of the Good.'

Although sin and evil can seem powerful and attractive, they are nowhere near as powerful and attractive as goodness. Yet it sometimes takes time to learn to love goodness, as it did for Augustine. Learning to put away pride, envy, greed and the rest is not an easy path to tread, but the whole direction of human life and destiny is working this way. Imagine wading into a river that is gently flowing towards the sea. As I step in, I suddenly find myself caught up in a small current, which because of the lie of the riverbed and the bend of the stream is flowing in the other direction, and I find it hard to keep my feet. Life today may feel a bit like being in that current. It may be hard to learn to live this way because the surrounding culture makes it difficult, but viewed from a distance, the whole river of human life and destiny lies in the other direction: the path of goodness and life and virtue.

Sin and Responsibility

One of the features we will revisit time and again in this book is the issue of how responsible we are for our sins. It's hard to talk about gluttony without touching on eating disorders, or to speak about sloth or 'spiritual despair' without mentioning depression. The borderline between patterns of behaviour for which we bear some responsibility and diseases of the mind, spirit and body over which we have little control can be very thin, and sometimes hard to find. However, this insight has always been part of Christian thinking about sin. Augustine developed an idea which has come to be known as 'original sin' and which helps to make sense of this complex area of human behaviour. His basic idea was that sin is not just a freely chosen act of brazen disobedience. Instead, we are biased in that direction before we even start. Our will, our capacity for choice, is not entirely free to choose exactly what it wants to do, but it has a tendency towards choosing the wrong direction, an inclination that comes from deep in the human past. So in one sense we are responsible for our own sins, yet in another we are not. We are caught in a network of relationships within the human race that means we do not start life with a blank slate.

In 2005 a boy aged twelve appeared in court in the UK, accused of raping his teacher. As the court case developed, the story emerged of a horrendous childhood. He was one of three brothers whose parents had divorced when he was two. By the age of four he had been abused and encouraged to drink alcohol and smoke cigarettes. His mother was an alcoholic and a heroin addict. She regularly beat her partner and screamed at her children. She would encourage men to get her drunk and take them home to have sex with her in front of the boys. She would often inject or smoke heroin in front of the children. The newspaper report read: 'The judge acknowledged that the boy's problems were not of his own making but said that nevertheless, he was very likely to commit further and equally serious offences.' The boy was convicted and given a three-year sentence.

This sadly common story illustrates the dilemma well. Was the boy responsible or not? Well, yes. And no. His behaviour is quite understandable when we think of his upbringing. Anyone brought up to think of women as objects and violence and drug abuse as normal is highly likely to end up acting out those very things. Yet it is not inevitable. A judge who acquitted such a person on the grounds of his upbringing would be howled down in protest, and quite rightly, as it would be a slur on all those who had endured such an upbringing and yet had resisted the path of violence and crime. So the boy is both guilty and not guilty. It is not purely his fault, but he is not solely to blame. That captures the human condition exactly. Sin always hovers in this area of responsibility and innocence, and it is sometimes hard to tell whether we are more sinned against or sinning. As we go through the book we will try to chart a way between these poles, recognizing when we are victims and when we are villains. The truth is we are all both.

Seven Deadly Sins?

So how do we begin thinking about sin? One traditional way is to classify it into types. Our ancestors shuddered at the thought of it, but they were shrewd enough to realize they needed to know their enemy. So the idea of the 'seven deadly sins' emerged as a neat way of remembering some of the chief ways in which this deadly pattern of behaviour manifested itself. The origins of the list are obscure. Some say they came from a list of eight bad habits drawn up by Evagrius of Pontus, a fourth-century Greek monastic theologian. Around 200 years later, while writing a book of reflections on the book of Job, the hugely influential Pope Gregory the Great reduced the list to seven, and the number stuck. The list has shifted over time, with the exact items and the order in which they come varying from one list to another, but it has caught our imagination as a tool to understand the moral life, or better, the immoral life.

By the time of the high middle ages, it had become a standard way of organizing sin – a useful taxonomy of misbehaviour. Perhaps the most famous treatment of all came in Dante's *Divine Comedy*, where he described his own dreamt expedition through hell, purgatory and heaven as a journey of exploration, purging and redemption from these seven fatal habits. Thomas Aquinas gave a classic analysis of the seven sins in his *De Malo* (On Evil), written in the 1270s, and used the list extensively in his great *Summa Theologiae*.

However, a glance through the traditional list of the seven deadly sins raises an obvious issue for anyone with any sense of contemporary life and morals: these are not the ones we would identify as the chief causes of evil in our world. If anything, our culture tends to admire these qualities, not avoid them. Lust is a sign of a healthy sexual appetite, pride a perfectly valid pleasure in our own achievements, and greed an essential motor for the economy. The philosopher Julian Baggini suggests that we jettison the old list and proposes a new one. His list comprises exploitation, dogmatism, righteousness, covetousness (at least one of the old candidates gets a place at the table!), vanity, complacency and thoughtlessness. For him it is these sins that lie at the heart of our current experience of evil. They are the culprits responsible for poverty, disease, discrimination and injustice.

Yet as we'll see on this journey through human

badness, the traditional list encompasses these, explains them and takes them deeper. Vanity and self-righteousness are symptoms of pride, the exaltation of self to an unopposed and delusional position of pre-eminence. Complacency and thoughtlessness both issue from the deeper malaise of sloth, a loss of passion for life, goodness and God. Exploitation of others is most often the result of uncontrolled lust or greed or gluttony, an out-of-proportion desire for sex, money or food at the expense of real people. At the same time, Baggini's dislike of dogmatism and 'thinking you are right while others are wrong' is deeply problematic. Does he think *he* is right in putting forward this list? Is he serious about making statements that make any sense at all? Of course the kind of dogmatism that refuses to think, to consider that it might be wrong or to engage in discussion or debate is unhealthy and damaging. Yet that doesn't mean we cannot hold opinions that we sincerely believe to be correct and choose to live our lives by them. Faith always has an element of doubt to it. To believe something we cannot prove (and most beliefs about God's existence or non-existence, the meaning of life and so on go beyond available proof) inevitably involves entertaining the possibility that we might be mistaken. Without that it would be certainty, not faith. But true faith is believing certain things to be true that we cannot ultimately prove, and choosing to live our lives by them. It is far from the dogmatism which we so fear.

The problem with such contemporary lists is that they tend to describe the symptoms, not the cause. They describe social or relational practices we don't like (such as exploitation, self-righteousness and thoughtlessness) without going very far towards explaining why we act in these ways. As we'll see, Christian reflection on human bad habits goes further in describing the kind of person who does these things, and the roots of such behaviour.

Such attempts to improve on the seven traditional sins often expose something of the shallowness of contemporary moral instincts, but then again that's not surprising. Such lists are the fruit of a few years' thought. The traditional list has been pondered and explored for around fifteen centuries, so I guess it has a bit of a head start. We might be wise in giving it our attention before throwing it away too soon, like the boy who found a Rembrandt in the attic and threw it away because it wasn't colourful enough.

Sin and God

Lust, anger and pride might get us what we want, but we'll end up enjoying it in perfect isolation, with a cancer eating at our soul and a deep loneliness all around. But the deepest sense of loneliness hits home at an even deeper level than losing friends and family. It results in being out of joint with the world and with God himself. It not only means being alone in our room, it means being alone in the universe. Sooner or later, when we're trying to understand how Christianity works, and how it can help us live a better and more fulfilled life, we have to face the question of God.

You may or may not think of yourself as a Christian and you may or may not believe in God. This book doesn't try to persuade you either way – that's for another day or another book, if it can be done at all. But I have to come clean at the start of this journey: however hard we try, the Christian life cannot be lived without God. We can't really begin to understand the Christian way of overcoming evil without God. However, we might be closer to this than we think. What led you to pick up a book like this? Perhaps a growing feeling of unease, a sense of guilt, a nagging fear that there's something wrong at the heart of your life, a desire to live a life that is better than the half-baked thing you are experiencing at the moment? If so, that is often a real sign that God is beginning to get to work on you. In the Bible, when people encountered God, they didn't usually have a feeling of harmony, love and universal peace. The encounter often started with a sense of deep inadequac – like the way a pub singer might feel if she came into the presence of a real diva, or a weekend golfer might feel if he played alongside a professional – only much, much greater. Isaiah the prophet, after he had experienced a vision of God in the temple, could only blurt out: 'Woe is me, for I am a man of unclean lips.' When Peter (later to be *St* Peter) saw Jesus begin to perform strange miracles, his reaction was to run as far as he could: 'Depart from me for I am a sinful man!' If we feel we need to change our life, or at least that it isn't what it ought to be, that might well be the first glimmer of the real God stirring something inside us. And that's a good sign, because for this to work, a relationship with God has to begin, however tentatively and shakily.

One last point. The aim of all this is not to draw up a list of rules to help us avoid sin. That would just be to revert to the toothless and moralizing approach of 'keeping the rules' that we touched on earlier. Instead the aim is to build a particular quality of life that enables us to weed out bad habits and build good ones. This is less like building a flat-pack set of bookshelves by following the instructions and more like learning to play the piano or getting fit. We don't read about it in a book and then just do what it says; we develop a skill, a quality of life that enables us to do certain things without even thinking about them. When we are physically fit, we can run for a bus and catch it, climb stairs without getting breathless and play tennis for an hour without turning purple and having a heart attack. Likewise when we are spiritually in shape, we can practice kindness, generosity and patience without even thinking about it. And we steer well clear of sloth, lust and envy just as we would a dead bird on the pavement.

However, it's never enough just to warn of evil. That way we are just left with a vacuum, an empty space. There is a parable in the Gospels to the effect that if all we do is drive out one demon, before we know it several others have come to take its place. Something more is needed: it is also necessary to point the path to goodness. So this book goes beyond trying to uncover the ugliness of sin to show how Christians, who originally identified this list, have dealt with it and found a way of building goodness or virtue. It aims to show how Christian faith offers a way of life that might enable us to overcome some really destructive habits and build some positive, constructive ones; in short, to help us live a better life, the kind of life we always hoped might be possible. This book tries to show how life might be different if we were not only to believe in God, but also to take seriously the possibility that he might be not just a concept in the mind, but a reality out there who actively seeks to teach us to live a different way.

In the end it is not our efforts that produce

virtue. The emergence of goodness in us is not a matter of strenuous moral exertion on our part, but of responding to the love of God, who looked for us long before we ever looked for him, and working together with the Holy Spirit, who tirelessly works to bring some likeness to Jesus Christ out of us, just as a sculptor works to bring a glorious statue out of a rough block of stone. The journey described in this book tries to show how we might work with him rather than against him in that process, and to highlight the pitfalls we want to avoid. Long ago, Dante wrote an account of a journey through the seven deadly sins on the path to virtue. So a journey like this has good precedents. It is not for the faint-hearted, but if we take it, we do not travel alone.

2 Pride

'I'm proud of you.' In their heart of hearts, that's what most children like to hear from their parents, husbands from their wives, workers from their bosses. We take pride in our work, our families, our achievements. We often appeal to children's sense of pride in themselves to encourage them to behave. We strive for status, and a sense of personal accomplishment promises security and pleasure. Being able to look back on our life with pride in our achievements is something we all aspire to. On the other hand, a sense of regret at not having made the best of ourselves is something we dread.

Yet when asked to rank sins, Christian moralists have tended to place pride at the top of the list. Augustine saw pride as the very thing that drew Satan away from God. The fallen angel then reproduced the same attitude of mind in humans, enticing them to be 'like gods'. In the *Divine Comedy*, when Dante and his companion enter purgatory, what is the first sin that needs to be purged? You guessed it. Thomas Aquinas thought the same: 'Inordinate self-love is the cause of every sin.' He was in no doubt that pride is the beginning of all sin: 'The root of pride is found to consist in man not being, in some way, subject to God and His rule.' In 1684, The Reverend William Master, a Gloucestershire vicar, was wondering how he might leave a lasting mark on his old university, Oxford. Perhaps to have a dig at what he considered its besetting sin, he bequeathed a sum to ensure that every subsequent year two sermons would be preached at the university: one on pride and one on humility. His wish is still observed to this day. G. K. Chesterton would have agreed: 'If I had only one sermon to preach it would be a sermon against pride.' T. S. Eliot adds his pennyworth: 'Most of the trouble in the world is caused by people wanting to be important.'

What it is about pride that so attracts the hostility

of these Christian writers and thinkers? After all, pride is not the most noticeable of faults. Drunkenness, lust, rage – wander into any city centre on a Saturday night and you will see plenty of evidence of these – but it's hard to spot open, naked, obvious pride.

Alain de Botton writes: 'There are four cardinal virtues today: creativity, courage, intelligence and stamina. The presence of other virtues, humility or godliness, for example, rarely detains attention.' He's right of course, yet it's not only our present culture that sees it this way. In fact in placing pride on the list, even at the head of the list, Christian morality shows itself to be at odds with other cultures as well. For Aristotle, for example, pride in one's city, family or nation was very definitely not only to be encouraged, but also one of the main motivations for good action. Humility might be the kind of stance appropriate towards the gods, but not towards a neighbour, and certainly not towards children or servants.

Pride and Self-esteem

Yet there is a genuine dilemma here. Christian advocacy of humility can seem a recipe for low self-esteem and a crippling inferiority complex. Psychological literature on the subject tends overwhelmingly to use the word 'pride' in a positive and approving manner. We are constantly told to take pride in ourselves, build a strong sense of self-esteem and so on. Is it wrong to do so?

The simple answer is no. But in order to understand this we need to distinguish between pride and self-esteem. It's not that self-esteem is wrong. It's more a question of how it is established. Is it attained by boosting my own sense of my own importance to myself and the world in general, or by some other route? Pride can seem the most obvious and sure-fire way to build a solid sense of self-worth. After all, if we want to feel good about ourselves, what could be more sensible than to remind ourselves as often as we can that we're not so bad after all, that all things considered we're decent, kind and thoughtful people, that we haven't committed any real crimes, at least not deliberately, and that we really wouldn't hurt a fly? The path suggested by Christian faith – that the best way to establish an unshakeable sense of self-worth is to go in exactly the opposite direction, refraining from such reveries and instead reminding ourselves of our faults, failings and mistakes – seems so odd, strange and counter-intuitive that it doesn't seem to make a lot of sense.

Jesus told a story which centres around two men, one a Pharisee, a very religious, good, respectable person, and the other a collector of Roman taxes – the first-century equivalent of a traffic warden, and not the most popular job you could choose (Luke 18:9–14). In a way, the story is about self-esteem and how it is established. The Pharisee takes the usual route to feeling good about himself. He recounts in his own mind (and before God of course) his own moral achievements, his very real devotion and discipline. He looks in the mirror and admits to himself that he can honestly say that he is not a bad person: 'God, I thank you that I am not like other men – robbers, evildoers, adulterers – or even like this tax collector. I fast twice a week and give a tenth of all I get.' This by any standard is impressive. If we met someone who did all those things we would surely conclude that here was a genuinely good person. He does not steal from others, never cheats on his wife, doesn't swear or gossip, and is generous to a fault. When we look at his life, he is undoubtedly *good*.

Yet all this goodness hides a subtle trap. We're not told why or how, but he has learnt to build his own sense of value on the foundation of his own goodness. It seems promising. He goes away from his time of prayer feeling good about himself, secure in his own worth. After all, he has not tried to justify himself by appealing to his money, status, power or looks – shallow things, of course, that other people might look to – no, he relies on things of real worth: his discipline, generosity and honesty, upstanding reputation and happy family life.

But in the story, Jesus says that however good the Pharisee felt about himself on his slow walk home from the temple, God did not see it that way. He did not go home 'justified before God'. This approach to building self-esteem never works in the long run. And it fails for two important reasons.

The first is that it is built on a very shaky foundation. It is like building an office block on land which is notoriously vulnerable to subsidence. It all looks good from the outside and works fine for a while – at least for as long as the Pharisee's moral achievement remains constant and nothing much goes wrong around him. But when out of the blue his wife tells him she has met someone else and wants a divorce, his eighteen-year-old son gets arrested for drug-dealing, or he himself ends up in court for drunk driving, his life comes crashing down. And with it comes his sense of his own worth. The rest of his life is dogged by regrets; a sense of failure and of a life lived among the ruins of pride.

Reputation is a very fragile thing. It can evaporate as quickly as dew on a summer's morning. Even a person's own belief in their essential good nature can be easily shaken. Do we really know what we might do when provoked? Can we really guarantee that we will not resort to lying through our teeth when it seems the only (and surely the most harmless) way to avoid shame and disgrace? And what about the dark secrets: the furtive gazing at porn, the sly, gossipy put-downs in a rival's absence? What if we stopped hushing up and making excuses for our dark secrets, and examined them steadily in the cold light of day?

Building self-worth through pride is a risky business. It works for a while, but we never know when it will all come tumbling down.

The second reason why this strategy of building self-esteem fails is hidden in the story Jesus tells. Bound up with the Pharisee's attempt to establish his own identity and worth through his moral achievement is an inevitable comparison of himself with everyone else, especially the rather grubby and embarrassing tax official praying in the other corner of the temple: 'I may not be perfect, but at least I'm better than him.' What results is a slight distancing, a tinge of superiority; a small but fatal break in the fundamental bond that unites him as a human being, and a frail, vulnerable, fallible one at that, with the man in the corner – his neighbour.

At its root, pride is the desire to look down on everyone else, or to put it differently, the refusal to recognize and admit the presence, equality or even superiority of any another being. In Milton's *Paradise Lost*, Satan is the archetype of pride. Having been cast out of heaven, he turns to Beelzebub his lieutenant, and says:

What though the field be lost?
All is not lost; the unconquerable will,
And study of revenge, immortal hate,
And courage never to submit or yield:

That glory never shall his wrath or might
Extort from me. To bow and sue for grace
With suppliant knee, and deify his power,
Who from the terror of this arm so late
Doubted his empire, that were low indeed
That were an ignominy and shame beneath
This downfall...

The last thing Satan will do is bow the knee to God, or anyone else for that matter. Hell may not be that pleasant, but at least there he is king – he defers to no-one. As he famously declares later:

Here we reign secure, and in my choice
To reign is worth ambition though in hell:
Better to reign in Hell, than serve in Heaven.

That is the essence of pride. Satan is pretty pleased with himself. He is on top of the pile in hell, rather than an also-ran in heaven. As Matt Damon's dark character in the film *The Talented Mr Ripley* says after murdering his friend and taking on his identity: 'It's better to be a fake somebody than a real nobody.' A proud woman would never say so of course, but secretly she thinks she deserves to look down on everyone else, because she knows she is more intelligent, better looking, more deserving, or perhaps less proud than anyone else she can think of.

And here we get to one of the key reasons why Christianity has it in for pride. If the essence of sin is that it renders us unable to build healthy relationships and societies, pride is the most isolating of all sins. There is a certain communality in mob anger and violence. Lust can be indulged in alone, but at least it sometimes involves another person. Sloth can be entertained with a good friend; quite a few unemployed flatmates have given up on life to watch endless hours of daytime TV, but at least they're doing it together. Yet pride is essentially competitive. Greed might become competitive if we go to a party, there's only one portion of pizza left and we have to get there before anyone else. But on the whole, greed isn't a competition. If there's enough to go round, then it doesn't set us against anyone else; it just damages our own body and soul.

Yet pride always sets up competition. As Henry Fairlie puts it: 'Pride must be competitive, since it cannot bear to concede first place to anyone else, even when its real wants are satisfied.' Because it is essentially competitive, it sets us against each other; it cannot do anything else. If greed is the desire to be rich, pride is the desire to be richer than everyone else. It means enmity; it makes me suspect my neighbour and compels me to put him down in all kinds of subtle and hidden ways, to make me appear or at least feel superior. The ultimate end of pride is loneliness. The worst thing that can happen to the proud person is to get exactly what he wants: to be the best, on top of the pile, better than anyone else, perfectly entitled to look down on them all, there in his castle, surrounded by his trophies and utterly alone. After all, who wants to spend their time with someone who is constantly dropping into conversations their own or their children's achievements and ignoring everyone else's? Very often that kind of behaviour emerges from a deep sense of insecurity, a desperate need to build self-esteem; it just goes about it the wrong way.

Lord, it's Hard to Be Humble...

So pride just doesn't work. But is humility any better? Humility can seem deeply unattractive, whether it's the smarmy, unctuous self-deprecation of a Uriah Heep, or a feeble, slightly pathetic attitude that certainly doesn't achieve anything in the real world of business, economics or politics. Of course it's possible, indeed very much so, to be proud of one's own humility. As someone once said: 'Humility is like underwear; essential, but indecent if it shows.'

So why is humility so vital? The answer is perhaps surprising. We are to learn humility not primarily because we need to learn our place, because we are miserable worms or sinful, worthless creatures, but so that we might be like God. We are to learn humility because God is humble.

Think of it this way. According to the Christian view of things, God is the most beautiful, wise, powerful, loving and gentle being there is. No-one else comes near. Is he therefore justified in being proud? Is pride acceptable for God and not for us? Our instinct tells us the answer has to be no, and our instinct is right. Jesus, as he is depicted in the Gospels and as he has been understood by Christians down the ages, is the perfect Son of God. But he was not proud. Instead he is portrayed as the most humble of men. There is a fascinating point in John's Gospel where the author emphasizes Jesus' status and origin, and then says something very surprising:

Jesus knew that the Father had put all things under his power, and that he had come from God and was returning to God; so he got up from the meal, took off his outer clothing, and wrapped a towel around his waist. After that, he poured water into a basin and began to wash his disciples' feet, drying them with the towel that was wrapped around him.

JOHN 13:3–5

We might expect John to say that *despite* the fact that Jesus had come from God, he took a towel and did the servant's job of washing the disciples' feet. The key word here, however, is the tiny word 'so'. It was precisely *because* he had all things under his power, came from God and so on that he performed this act of utter humility.

In other words, God is humble, even though he does not appear to have that much to be humble about. He doesn't draw attention to himself, and doesn't shout about his own qualities. Instead he leaves it to others to do that for him. This fits with the way the world is made. If I had been the creator of all that exists, I would have made sure that the credit went where it was deserved. Yet the world around us has precious few explicit reminders of God. There is no unmistakeable signature written in the sky, no billboards or flashing neon lights saying 'Made by God, just for YOU!'. In fact it is quite possible to go through life and completely miss God altogether.

If there is a God, he seems oddly reticent and unwilling to advertise his existence, or as the prophet Isaiah put it, perhaps in a moment of frustration many centuries ago, 'Truly, you are a God who hides himself' (Isaiah 45:15). This theme of the 'hidden God' has fascinated theologians and philosophers from the apostle Paul to Martin Luther, and from Blaise Pascal to Søren Kierkegaard. Pascal was especially fascinated by the strange hiddenness of God, and explained it by arguing that God hides himself so that he cannot be found by the idly curious, but only by those who seek him with all their hearts, or whose nature is pure enough to see him: 'He is a God so pure that he can only be discovered by those whose hearts have been purified.'

When God does reveal himself, in the arrival on the human scene of Jesus Christ, even then he is oddly hidden. Jesus was again perplexingly reluctant to identify himself as God. By and large he didn't go around saying, 'Look at me, I am divine!' It was possible to meet Jesus of Nazareth face to face, and go away thinking he was just another Jewish rabbi or miracle-worker. In fact, he was more likely to be found acting out the role of a servant – washing the feet of his friends, providing them with food, living a wandering, homeless existence and dying on a criminal's cross – than doing important things such as wearing robes, exerting political power or living in palaces. Nowhere does God appear to us unmistakeably. He is not an in-your-face kind of God. He seems, odd though it is to say it, quite shy. Or perhaps the best word is simply 'humble'.

It's not a quality we normally associate with gods, but if it is true that the God of the Christians is humble, then it is an important clue for us on our journey. On the one hand it gives us the deepest reason why pride is fatal, and on the other, it tells us more of what humility is.

We are to be humble because God our creator is humble. If God is not proud, then why on earth would we want to be? In the Christian view of things, we were created in the image of God, to be like him. Not, of course, with unlimited power; thankfully we are not entrusted with that, and heaven knows what we would do with it if we were. Yet we are made to reflect his characteristics of love, compassion, wisdom, goodness, generosity, patience, forgiveness and, of course, humility. We are at our most fully human when we are most like God, which of course is why the early Christians concluded that Jesus, the most God-like person the world had ever seen, was both fully God and fully human. In pride we think to raise ourselves, to make ourselves seem more important, more exalted. Yet the paradox is that it is humility that makes us more like God. As Augustine put it: 'It was pride that changed angels into devils; it is humility that makes men as angels.'

This also fills out our picture of what it means to be humble. If pride is wanting everyone to notice us and look up to us, humility is being secure enough not to draw attention to ourselves all the time, giving space for other people or things to exist and be themselves, refusing to impose ourselves and our agenda on others, and leaving them the opportunity to grow and flourish with or without us. It is the willingness and the ability to be the servant of others; to be more interested in hearing the stories or successes of others than in reciting our own. Just like God.

Pride, Humility and Worship

But at this point a problem arises. What about worship? What about those bits of the Bible where we are told to praise God, bow down before him and submit to his will? Is that because he likes being told how great he is? Is it because, after all, he's just like us, craving the adulation and devotion of as many people as possible? Is God secretly proud?

In one of the Psalms, the author reflects upon the elaborate sacrificial worship of the Israelites, and puts these words into the mouth of God:

I have no need of a bull from your stall or of goats
from your pens,
For every animal of the forest is mine, and the cattle
on a thousand hills.
I know every bird in the mountains, and the creatures
of the field are mine.
If I were hungry I would not tell you for the world is
mine, and all that is in it.
Do I eat the flesh of bulls or drink the blood of
goats?

PSALM 50:9–13

In other words, God has no need of human worship. He does not crave it like a despot who desperately needs worship to bolster his fragile ego. God is perfectly self-sufficient. Yet he is not lonely. The

Christian idea of God as Trinity, or three in one, which we have come across before, says that God has community in his very being. We might imagine God as a solitary figure, moping over his own isolation and suddenly deciding to create a world of tiny human creatures to keep him company, like some lonely old man who buys a dog to take the edge off his solitude. Yet nothing could be further from the God we're talking about. He does not need our worship, but we begin to discover that it is in fact good for us. The reason we are to praise God is not for his sake but for ours.

Worshipping something or someone other than ourselves is salutary. It takes our attention off ourselves for once and focuses it elsewhere. That is the first step of worship: a good start, helping us lose our self-fascination. Yet if the object of our worship is tainted, then it does not take us very far. To worship ourselves is folly, because we are mixed bags of goodness and evil, altruism and selfishness, beauty and ugliness. To worship another human being who seems a bit better than us might seem a good idea, but the reality is they are probably much the same as we are.

We need to find the best thing possible to worship for one simple reason, which the biblical authors often identify: we become like the things we worship. One of the poets behind the book of Psalms takes a satirical look at the common practice in neighbouring cultures of the ancient Near East of worshipping man-made statues of the gods:

The idols of the nations are silver and gold,
made by the hands of men.
They have mouths, but cannot speak,
eyes, but they cannot see;
They have ears but cannot hear,
nor is there breath in their mouths.
Those who make them will be like them,
and so will all who trust in them.

PSALM 135:15–18

It's perhaps a cheap shot by the Psalmist, but it contains more than a grain of truth. We become like the object of our worship, whether it is a group of friends we spend all our time with or a celebrity whom we try to imitate as far as possible. If that's true then we want to learn to worship the very best. And that is why we are invited to worship God, the one who is full of love, grace and humility. As we learn to make a habit of joining in worship of him, slowly but surely we become like him.

Pride, Humility and Community

There is an old story of a man who had a dream. In the dream he visited hell, which consisted of a room with a large table in the centre. Sitting around the table were many guests, and the table was laden with all kinds of delicious food; yet the diners were angry, miserable and hungry, and a sullen silence hung in the room. As he looked, he discovered the reason. Each of them was seated too far away from the table to reach it, so they had all been given a very long spoon. Yet although they could now pick up the food, the spoon was too long for them to put it into their own mouths. So everyone went hungry.

The man was then taken to heaven, where to his surprise, the same scene was repeated. Yet here there was laughter, joy and lively conversation. As he watched he soon understood why. Here, instead of trying to wedge their long spoon into their own mouths, each person had learnt to use it to feed someone else seated a little further away. This way everyone was fed and everyone was happy.

This is a parable of the way we are made: to be servants of one another. When we have learnt that vital but deeply counter-intuitive skill, human community simply works. It is hard to learn to be the servant of someone else. It doesn't come naturally to us. And it is pride that is the chief obstacle. Pride will never let us be a servant; it will always make us want to be the master of our own fate, the king of our own destiny, beholden to no-one.

Pride alienates us from each other; humility binds

us together. That is why it is such a vital art to learn. It is why the wisest Christians have tended to stick close to servants, and the poor in general, rather than the rich, powerful and influential. If we want to learn to be servants of one another, we may have more to learn from the former than the latter.

Humility also builds self-esteem in a much more effective way than pride. Christian humility takes its cue from God, and finds its security in being created, loved and forgiven by God. It is like a child who, as she grows, knows that whatever she does, her mother loves her, will never abandon her and is always there to return to when everything falls apart. That child is likely to grow up secure and less anxious to prove herself, with a more settled sense of value, than one who has no such refuge, no loving parent to give her identity and a true home. Martin Luther once wrote: 'We are not loved because we are attractive, we are attractive because we are loved.' That is the secret of the Christian approach to self-esteem: avoiding the tempting route of pride, keeping up the façade of niceness and I-never-hurt-anybody-really harmlessness, and instead finding a sense of value simply in being loved by God. And that takes some humility.

Humility can seem weak and passive. In fact it is the most powerful force in the world. It binds the broken; it softens the hardest of hearts; it defeats every enemy. As Father Zosima says in Dostoyevsky's *The Brothers Karamazov*:

At some thoughts a man stands perplexed, above all at the sight of human sin, and he wonders whether to combat it by force or by humble love. Always decide 'I will combat it by humble love'. If you resolve on that once for all, you can conquer the whole world. Loving humility is a terrible force: it is the strongest of all things, and there is nothing like it.

Overcoming Pride

So how do we defeat pride and learn the delicate and necessary art of humility? Two classic Christian disciplines are the beginning of the road to humility.

The first is what Christians call confession. Of course this flies in the face of all self-help manuals and how-to-succeed-in-life books. But unless we cultivate a habit of self-examination, regularly reminding ourselves that we often boast, tell small untruths, take the easy way out, and fail to love our wife/husband, our children, our friends (let alone our enemies), and that difficult neighbour down the road as we know we should, we will always keep thinking that we're OK, that we've not done anything wrong, and we will start to believe it. Here is one area in which we are not like God. God doesn't have any faults to remind himself of, so he doesn't need to do this. But then again he's not tempted to selfish pride in the way we are, so he doesn't need it in the way that we do. Confession doesn't mean wallowing in self-hatred. A constant state of self-laceration over faults, real or perceived, is not healthy, nor is it what is meant by confession. We are meant to have a healthy sense of self-worth, deriving from the knowledge that we are deeply loved by our creator. But every once in a while, maybe once a day, we can reflect on where we took the wrong option and admit it to ourselves and to God. This habit of confession is a sure-fire way of avoiding pride. It is the one way to ensure we do not try to become little gods.

The second discipline is service. When we learn to serve someone else, to do something which would normally be beneath us, it has the effect of helping us forget ourselves. Humility is not absent-mindedness; as C. S. Lewis once put it, 'Humility is thinking less *about* yourself, not thinking less *of* yourself.' It isn't telling ourselves that we're useless, a waste of space, better off dead and so on. More often than not that is self-pity. It doesn't mean lying about our qualities, gifts, abilities and achievements. The truly humble person isn't always telling people how humble they really are. Dickens' Uriah Heep, who is constantly saying what a humble and unworthy person he is, is not humble at all; in fact he is deeply proud, as we can tell from the fact that he is always talking about himself and his own humility. Humble people are not self-haters, they just don't think about themselves much – they are far more interested in other people.

So the first step in a Christian approach to learning goodness is to refuse to be a little god and set myself up as king of all I survey, the most important person in my own little world. It means stepping down from my throne and admitting that I need other people and that others' claims are as important as my own. But of course if I do that, it leaves an empty throne in my heart and soul, and it is vital to decide well what should fill that throne. Filling it with another person, a passion for skiing, a football team or a career ambition is just not worth it. That throne is made only for our creator, and only when he begins to take that place do we truly start to discover the deep wisdom of God in how to live. And the first thing we may need to learn is how to respond to the good things he provides in his world. In other words, we start learning how to deal with the next great sin: envy.

3 Envy

Out of all the sins, envy is different. It is different because it is the one sin on the list that has no pleasure in it whatsoever. From start to finish, envy is no fun at all. It is the most miserable of habits. Just about all the others can be enjoyed at least for a while. Even the most pious have to admit the promised pleasures of lust, or the relief that comes from letting go a pent-up tirade of anger against someone who has riled us. Gluttony tastes excellent for a while, pride makes us feel good about ourselves, greed entices us with a vision of expensive holidays and fast cars, and sloth does let us stay in bed longer. But no-one chooses to spend their time secretly delighting in a secret bout of covetousness. Henry Fairlie said this about envy: 'Its appetite never ceases, yet its only satisfaction is endless self-torment.' Gregory the Great described the envious man as 'so racked by another's happiness, that he inflicts wounds on his own pining spirit'. Envy is self-harm, self-abuse that no-one would ever choose, yet when it takes hold, is hard to shake off. Has anyone ever actually enjoyed being envious?

Envy is described in various ways, but most definitions come back to something like that of the eighth-century monk and theologian John of Damascus: 'Envy is discontent over someone else's blessings'; or that of Thomas Aquinas: 'sadness at the happiness or glory of another'. Envy is closely tied to discontent with our own lot, while at the same time looking at someone else's and wishing it were ours. To feel envy is to have a gnawing, aching pain eating away at our insides. It leaves us no peace, and takes away all pleasure in the things we might otherwise have enjoyed. Imagine Catherine constantly looking across the office at her colleague, Frances, thinking how much more stunningly successful, beautiful and interesting Frances is. However successful, beautiful and interesting Catherine is on the broader scale of things, her own job, looks or personality will still taste insipid and bland. Catherine might actually score quite highly on these features to most outside observers, but while she is consumed with envy for Frances she will be unable to enjoy her own good fortune. A man might enjoy his own home as comfortable and spacious, with a decent kitchen, beers in the fridge and room enough for the family and the dog. But when he goes next door and sees his neighbour with a bigger house, larger garden, two extra bedrooms, a pool table and a dedicated TV room, complete with 40-inch plasma screen and surround sound, somehow his own house seems pale and boring. When he returns home, he is no longer able to enjoy it as he once did.

It is in part perhaps for this reason that envy has remained on the list of serious sins even in the twenty-first century. Our age struggles to see what's wrong with a bit of harmless lust, proper pride and justified anger. Sloth and gluttony seem like unfortunate personality traits rather than serious sins. But envy: well, that's a different matter. Because envy is no fun, we simply hate it.

There are several reasons for our continued despising of envy. The philosopher Julian Baggini argues that our moral compass has shifted dramatically so that acts of wrongdoing are defined more as 'offences against human life' than acts against a higher being such as God. This explains, he says, the enduring hatefulness of envy: 'Of the seven deadly sins, only envy and anger still retain some edge of wickedness. We can clearly see that these are not only bad in the eyes of God… but bad for us.' He contrasts this with what he considers the root of the older Christian view of sin: the idea that we are destined for another life, and therefore not really meant to enjoy this one. His understanding of contemporary culture is better than his understanding of Christianity: on a Christian view of things, sins are indeed offences against human life, yet they are even more serious because they are also offences against the God who made that life in the first place. Moreover, Christians are commanded to enjoy this world as God's good creation. Sins are bad in the eyes of Christian writers, not because they make us enjoy this world too much, but because they stop us from enjoying it properly and responsibly. However, despite these flaws, Baggini has at least put his finger on one of the key features of envy. It is perhaps the sin that displays most clearly sin's destructive, damaging character: it is just a waste of time.

Another reason for our contemporary dislike of envy is less flattering: it just doesn't look good. To be angry can be seen as self-assertive, lust indicates virility or seductive power, and sloth presents itself as a laid-back, ironic detachment from fanaticism. Yet no-one wants to be known as envious. Envy makes us feel smaller than other people. It seems just a bit pathetic, the sin of the inadequate or the failure. The novelist Zadie Smith writes:

That the concept of envy as a sin should retain its weight despite the present debilitation of the church and God himself is, I think, a part of our contemporary solipsism. We don't mind being seen to be angry or lustful or even lazy, but we dislike being seen as envious. It is unattractive. And our vanities superseded our virtues some time ago.

Envy remains thoroughly unenviable.

An Epidemic of Envy

We might think, then, that with our recognition of the unpleasantness of envy, our culture would have set its face against it in every possible way. Yet incitement to envy is everywhere. It is 'the key behind every advertisement', as the *Travellers' Guide to Hell* by Dana Facaros and Michael Pauls puts it. Envy is a powerful driving force behind the economy of most developed and developing countries. Where would most marketing departments be if they were not allowed to appeal to envy in their promotion of their products? And where would our ever-expanding economies be without the advertisers who entice us to consume those products? Of course it is possible to buy and enjoy good things without a trace of envy, but it would take a brave person to claim that they had never bought anything out of a desire to match a friend, sister or work colleague. A key reason for buying an 'ultra-sharp 30-inch wide-screen black flat panel monitor, LCD with height-adjustable stand' is that it will become 'an object of envy for your friends'. A car is advertised by its main attractive features: 'Performance, reliability and... envy'. Envy may not be very desirable, but the ability to inspire it in (or inflict it on) others definitely is. As Mark Twain put it: 'A man will do many things to get himself loved; he will do all things to get himself envied.'

The other feature of contemporary culture that breeds envy is of course the epidemic of hunger for fame. Celebrity culture is essentially a world of envy, depicting a procession of people who exhibit some quality or other that is thought to be desirable, whether looks, acting talent, sporting ability, or even in a strange self-parody, just fame itself. There are celebrities who are famous for being famous. The volume of applicants for reality TV shows testifies to people's huge craving for recognition or even notoriety, for Andy Warhol's celebrated fifteen minutes of fame. The cult of celebrity is a symptom of a chronic and whining narcissism, a way of grabbing attention, of making everyone else sit up and take notice. Perhaps behind the desire to be in the gossip columns is a small childish voice saying, 'Look at me, take notice of me, envy me!'

The reason for this epidemic of envy is not hard to find. In pre-modern times, societies were more rigidly hierarchical and people tended to accept their place in them. Today, Western societies are essentially meritocratic. In theory at least, it is possible for anyone to aspire to wealth or power. Boundaries of class, geography and gender are no longer as fixed as they were. We are all supposed to be equals now, all starting from the same point. In the sixteenth century, a peasant didn't envy a prince. They lived in different worlds and there was no possibility that the peasant could ever end up transcending such iron-hard social boundaries. Today, however, a greater sense of social equality has brought huge benefits, but an unfortunate downside is a greater potential for envy to rear its head. We are all within reach of one another, and so we resent those who have done better than us, thinking that if only things had been different, we might have had that person's job/car/wife/husband. As Alain de Botton puts it in his book, *Status Anxiety*:

The more people we take to be our equals, and compare ourselves to, the more people there will be to envy... the price we have paid for expecting to be so much more than our ancestors is a perpetual anxiety that we are far from being what we might be.

So perhaps envy has a paradoxical status as both the most hated and the most cultivated of all sins in the contemporary world. We are caught in a culture that hates envy, yet incites it mercilessly. We don't like to be envious but our whole way of life is built upon it.

This does mean that I probably don't have to work hard in this chapter to persuade anyone that envy is a bad thing. Trying to argue that chastity is preferable to lust is going to be a tough one, I know. Yet pitting envy against contentment is no contest. Given the choice, no-one in their right mind would choose to be consumed with envy rather than possess a settled contentment with life.

True, there is a potentially positive edge to envy; comparing ourselves to others can be a spur to achievement and an antidote to giving up on life too easily. But even then it's questionable how advisable it is as a motivation for aspiration. There are other and better reasons for wanting to achieve – to relieve the suffering of others, or to provide good things for one's family or community, for example. Striving to better ourselves just to be on a par with our colleagues or competitors or even to outdo them might get us going, but in the long run it is likely to isolate us and leave us with few friends.

The question is how to avoid envy, or conversely, how to develop contentment. There is an old saying that happiness consists not in getting what we want, but in wanting what we get. To be truly content with what life has dealt us, to envy no-one and to be satisfied with who we are, is a sublime and desirable thing. But how do we cultivate contentment? To answer that question requires delving a little deeper into the roots of envy.

Murder and Envy

There is a story in the book of Genesis that could claim to be one of the earliest written on the theme of envy: the story of Cain and Abel. These are two brothers, said to be the sons of Adam and Eve. They are both farmers: Cain, the elder, working on the land; Abel with livestock. They come before God with their offerings, and God accepts Abel's offering but rejects Cain's. Cain is understandably angry at this development, and despite an extended conversation with God over the matter, he harbours a growing resentment against his more successful brother, inveigles Abel out onto his land, the place where he, Cain, is master, and murders him. As a result, God banishes Cain from the land, condemning him to be a lost soul all his life: 'a restless wanderer on the earth'.

The story is told with typical biblical simplicity. It is brief, economical and evocative. Questions are left unanswered and details are few. Why does God not accept Cain's offering? We are not told. Commentators and translators have tried to suggest that Abel offered the best, whereas Cain offered the leftovers. It's hard to pin much on that, though; it's much more likely that we're not told the reason deliberately. The fact that we don't know why adds to the poignancy and immediacy of the story. Often when we look at someone else who seems to have a better deal in life than us, there isn't an obvious reason we can point to. It's not that they have deserved it and we haven't. In fact the other person might be an unmitigated scoundrel, which adds to the sense of injustice. This aspect of the story – our incomprehension as to why Abel gets favoured over Cain – is somehow true to our experience of life, which doesn't always work out fairly.

Cain's experience is universal. He is the firstborn, the one who, he would assume, has a right to expect preferential treatment. He looks at his brother across the village and every time he sees him a nagging anger grows that this is just not right. Why was he favoured and not me? That thought is so often the beginning of disaster. We sense an unfairness in life. Why is it that I have worked so hard and kept the rules, and yet my brother/sister/colleague/friend seems to get the best jobs, the best partners, earns more money or has fewer hassles in their life? I remember a young man coming to me as his pastor and pouring his heart out. He was single and had recently met a woman. She was wonderful, kind, clever and beautiful. When they were together they seemed to get on so well, sharing all kinds of interests and tastes. The only problem was that she was already married. Not only that, she was married to someone whom this man felt didn't appreciate or deserve her. Why hadn't he met her earlier? Why was this relationship, which seemed so right, barred forever? Why had life, fate, God or whoever it was dealt him such a tough hand?

The author of the story of Cain, in a moment of piercing perceptiveness, indicates that before Cain is angry with Abel, he is angry with God:

So Cain was very angry, and his face was downcast. Then the Lord said to Cain: 'Why are you angry?'

GENESIS 4:5

This is always the way envy works. It never starts with the object of envy. It starts with a shake of the fist at the skies, a frustration with the gods, a deep feeling of injustice. Why has God not given me what I want, or need, or deserve? Only then is Cain's anger directed at Abel, a more tangible and visible target for his fury. Discontent leads to envy, envy to murder and murder to the destruction of two lives: Abel's and Cain's, who is doomed to be a restless wanderer for what remains of his life.

The story has been played out often. Antonio Salieri was an eighteenth-century composer who had a tangled relationship with his younger contemporary, Wolfgang Amadeus Mozart. Rumours abounded at the time of jealousy and bitterness between them, even going as far as to suggest that Salieri was responsible for Mozart's death. The stories were exaggerated, but they were enough for the playwright Peter Shaffer to depict the relationship as one of intense jealousy on the part of the mediocre Salieri towards the genius of the younger man. The 1984 film by Milos Forman of Shaffer's play *Amadeus* has Salieri looking back on his life from a lunatic asylum, driven mad by envy of Mozart's gifts, talents given to someone he deems a shameless, irreverent, frivolous youth. Salieri is torn between wonder at the aching beauty of Mozart's music, and loathing for this rogue whose gifts so outshine his own:

I heard the music of true forgiveness filling the theatre, conferring on all who sat there, perfect absolution. God was singing through this little man to all the world, unstoppable, making my defeat more bitter with every passing bar.

Here too, the real argument is with God. Why has he given such gifts to someone so unworthy, and not the proper, upstanding and respectable Salieri, who has desperately prayed for the ability to be a great composer, promising to give God his devotion, work, chastity and life? Yet God has not answered his prayer. At one point, addressing a crucifix, Salieri speaks directly to God:

From now on we are enemies, you and I. Because you choose for your instrument a boastful, lustful, smutty, infantile boy and give me for reward only the ability to recognize the incarnation. Because you are unjust, unfair, unkind, I will block You, I swear it. I will hinder and harm your creature on earth as far as I am able.

Like Cain, Salieri's real problem is not with Mozart, it is with God. That is where the roots of envy lie. And that is where the remedy for envy must begin.

Envy and God

In the story of Cain and Abel, while Cain is smouldering in his anger, God addresses him:

Why are you angry? Why is your face downcast? If you do right, will you not be accepted? But if you do not do what is right, sin is crouching at your door; it desires to have you, but you must master it.

GENESIS 4:6–7

The perception of injustice, of unfair treatment, places a dilemma before Cain. At this point in the story, Cain has not yet done anything wrong. Just to feel that life is unfair, to be angry at the way in which unworthy people seem to get a better deal than those we think deserve it more (like ourselves, of course), is not in itself wrong. Sin has not yet taken hold of Cain, yet it lies in wait for him, ready to pounce, precisely at this moment. He can either indulge it and allow his sense of pique to lead him into hatred and malice, or he can take another route: to 'do what is right'. He can turn away from God in resentment, convinced that he knows best and God doesn't. Or he can turn back, engage God in conversation, struggle to understand and to trust. It is significant in the story that after God has spoken to Cain, Cain does not reply. He merely turns away, goes straight to Abel and invites him for a deadly walk in the fields. Cain has no intention of trying to understand God's ways. He just doesn't want to know; he doesn't want to listen. He has set his heart against God and so inevitably against Abel as well.

So the first step in dealing with envy is to turn back to the very God who seems to have treated us so badly. It is counter-intuitive; after all, it does seem as if it's God who is the problem – he hasn't ordered life in the way he should have. It is to try to begin to understand a different way of looking at the world, to view the world as far as we can from a different perspective: God's perspective.

Is God to Blame?

The first thing the Christian faith says at this point is very important: *not everything happens because God wants it to happen.* There is a kind of popular theology that attributes every event, every desire, everything that happens, to an 'Act of God'. Christians on the other hand believe that, although the world is good because it has been created by God, it is now fallen, broken, and no longer works in the way it was originally intended. It is like when a computer is affected by a virus: it still works after a fashion and can still be used and even remedied with the right treatment, but all kinds of things within the computer malfunction or fail to work in the original manner.

Therefore, if sickness afflicts me while my neighbour enjoys perfect health, I am not to conclude that it happened because God chose to strike me down and to leave the man next door untouched. When a person loses their job, a child dies of leukaemia, or a nation starves because of famine, Christian theology doesn't draw the immediate conclusion that God did all these things. The world as Christians understand it is a complex mixture of good and evil, or of the original design and the effects of the evil that has entered into the world.

God could of course remove all causes of evil from the world tonight, if he chose. Yet, attractive as it sounds, would we really want him to do that? If he did, it would involve removing me and removing you. Instead he leaves our twisted hearts be, with good and evil in his world growing together like weeds tangled around a beautiful rose, working slowly but surely to disentangle them by taking ordinary people like the one writing this book and the one reading it, and turning them into part of the solution, rather than part of the problem.

So good and evil live alongside each other in this world, at least for the time being, waiting for the day when evil will be defeated once and for all. One day, these two things will be separated and evil banished back to where it belongs; but until then things will happen in God's world that God did not initiate. This perspective makes a difference when it comes to dealing with envy. Unlike Cain or Salieri, I don't need to get angry with God when bad things happen to me – much less when good things happen to my neighbour. Rather than getting angry with God, which leads nowhere (or, rather, to murder in Cain's case and madness in Salieri's), we can begin to take another approach, which sees God as the solution rather than the problem.

Dealing with Envy 1: Changing the Price Tags

Why is it that we think a person is better off because they are rich, have a particular configuration of facial features that we consider more attractive than others, or have a job with more responsibility and status? At the heart of Christian faith is the idea that God's ways are not the same as ours. The prophet Samuel realizes this when he is choosing a king for Israel: 'The Lord does not look at the things man looks at. Man looks at the outward appearance, but the Lord looks at the heart' (1 Samuel 16:7).

Martin Luther, the sixteenth-century reformer, went through a great deal of questioning during his early career as a monk and an academic theologian. He struggled with the idea of God's approval and forgiveness: if God liked those who were morally good, who achieved some standard of righteousness, what did that say to those like him who were far too conscious of their own moral and spiritual failings? After intense study of scripture and the works of theologians from the early church, he came to the conclusion that God does not do what we might expect: approve of the good, the upright and those who seem on the surface to be fine upstanding pillars of society, who always do their best. Instead, he forgives and reaches out to those who know they have not done their best, who know they are far from what they could be, and who are looked down on by most others as failures. As the apostle Paul says, God 'justifies the ungodly', not the godly. Luther puts the same idea a different way: 'God only saves sinners, only teaches the stupid, only enriches the poor, only raises the dead.' So contrary to what we normally think, it is best to know that we are stupid, poor and, spiritually at least, moribund.

Luther then worked this insight through the rest of his theology and realized that the implications were huge. To put it bluntly, we usually misunderstand God's ways. God tends to do things differently from the way we expect. So rather than assuming we know best, we should not jump too quickly to conclusions about what God is or is not doing, but instead realize that, as Luther writes elsewhere, '*Aliter habet quam apparet*', which roughly translates as 'Things are not what they seem.' Things that seem weak are often in reality very strong; what is despised by most people can turn out to be the most prized of all; and in particular, the experience of suffering that we all dread the most can sometimes, despite its pain, be the most valuable and salutary.

The apostle Paul went through a similar process. He seems to have suffered from some kind of physical ailment, perhaps a problem with his sight. He was also unfavourably compared with some other travelling preachers in the early Christian world; he was not a particularly good communicator and did not on first impression strike people as someone worth listening to. Perhaps he was small, had a whining voice and came over a bit intense. Yet as he reflects on this, he senses God telling him that his very weakness is the means by which God's power will mysteriously be at work in and through him:

The Lord said to me: 'My grace is sufficient for you, for my power is made perfect in weakness.' Therefore I will boast all the more gladly about my weaknesses, so that Christ's power may rest on me.

2 CORINTHIANS 12:9

The paradigm for all this is the death of Christ. In one sense, the picture of Jesus dying on a cross is perhaps the strongest argument for atheism the world has seen. Here is the best man who ever lived, and yet God seems to abandon him to die a gruesome and cruel death. If ever there was a picture of injustice, this is it. Yet to the eye of faith, in some mysterious way, Christians insist that through the death of Christ on the cross, God was rescuing the world, doing what it took to ensure forgiveness and 'reconciling the world to himself', as Paul puts it. This most ugly and despicable event was transformed into the most wonderful act of love and grace. The cross became beautiful.

Both Paul and Luther are able to grasp a reversal of values, so that what might seem valuable in most people's eyes in is reality of little value, and what is usually disdained is in fact of real and lasting worth. Perhaps fame, financial security and apparent success in work are not the most important things to strive for? Perhaps there are things that can be gained through the experience of sickness that can never be learnt though good health? Perhaps public shame can be the road to real self-discovery, to realizing for once what matters and what doesn't?

This is one of the main Christian ways of dealing with envy: to begin to question the system of values that says we should envy the wealthy, famous and beautiful. If God's ways are different from ours, if he looks on the heart and not the outward appearance, if he works out his will through his own experience of death on the cross of Jesus, then maybe wealth, fame and good looks are not all they are cracked up to be, and wasting our time envying people who happen to have them is simply foolish. The ability to love, to build friendships and to be content, for example, is far more valuable than these. They are the qualities to strive for, the ones that satisfy more deeply than money, sex and fame. To begin to grasp this reversal of values is to begin to loosen the grip of envy on our souls.

Dealing with Envy 2: The Value of Gifts

The second Christian approach to envy is to learn to admire without comparing. Envy is a mixture of admiration and distaste, wonder and revulsion, love and hate. Salieri both adored and detested Mozart's music. Usually, envy involves seeing something in someone else that I don't possess but would like for myself, and resenting that person for having it in the first place. The trick is to admire the person, or the quality the person has, without envying them.

The way Christian faith does this is to separate the person from the ability, and to think of our abilities not as things we possess, have learnt or deserve, but instead as *gifts*. If the ability to play the piano with passion, to play golf with a single-figure handicap or to understand complex mathematical equations is a gift, then it implies a giver – someone who created and donated this ability from the outside. Christian theology thinks of people first and foremost as simple, elemental beings, who are given gifts or personal qualities, and who are never to forget that these are gifts and not possessions. The Old Testament character Job dramatically endures a sudden series of disasters, losing his family, his livelihood and his possessions. His response encapsulates the approach of the Judeo-Christian approach to the human person: 'Naked I came from my mother's womb, and naked I shall depart. The Lord gave and the Lord has taken away, may the name of the Lord be praised' (Job 1:20).

This way of thinking helps us see that whatever ability another person has (or that we have, for that matter) is not theirs, something they can be proud of, but a gift given to them. If there is any credit attached to it, then that belongs to God and not to them. Naturally there is an element of hard work that goes into developing a gift of playing the cello or cricket, but often strangely we don't envy people the result of such endeavours, because we know that we could do the same if we chose. The bit we feel envious about is the natural ability, the aptitude in the first place.

So part of the secret of overcoming envy is to learn to see people as Job saw himself: as essentially poor, naked, vulnerable and empty, yet also endowed with gifts that are not deserved or merited. That makes it just a little easier to acknowledge and enjoy the gift without feeling resentful of the person.

The other aspect of Christian faith that helps here is its very communal understanding of human life. When the New Testament writers talk of personal gifts, they see them as given not first and foremost to the individual, but primarily to the community. A gift is given to one person for the good of everyone else, and gifts are ranked according to how useful they are to other people. A gift that is purely for my own benefit (an example in the earliest Christian churches was the ability to speak in a spiritual language called 'tongues') is of little value compared with gifts that are of benefit to everyone else (such as the ability to speak words of wisdom, encouragement and challenge to the whole group).

Envy is a selfish emotion. It makes me resent the fact that someone else can play wonderful music, wishing instead that I could do it. Imagine a culture with a more communal understanding of human life than ours, where the emphasis is much more on the community than the individual, the good of the whole rather than the separate parts. People living in such a world would tend to be happy that the music existed, that at least someone among them could produce such awe-inspiring sounds rather than no-one being able to do it. They would hardly notice who actually had the ability and who didn't; what matters is that the human race has it at all.

Dealing with Envy 3: Connecting with God

The apostle Paul at one point writes this:

I have learned to be content whatever the circumstances. I know what it is to be in need, and I know what it is to have plenty. I have learned the secret of being content in any and every situation, whether well fed or hungry, whether living in plenty or living in want.

PHILIPPIANS 4:11–12

What is his secret? As we have seen, happiness and contentment are comparative things. A man can be happy with a stale loaf of bread if he has been cold, hungry and naked, whereas another can be deeply unhappy with a three-course meal in a nice restaurant if he is consumed with envy of his neighbour, who has a five-course meal in an even more exclusive restaurant.

So the secret of contentment is to have something that cannot be taken away and that no-one can better. Christianity says this is what is found in a bond with God through Jesus Christ. Paul says, directly after his statement about contentment, 'I can do everything through him who gives me strength.' Of course he doesn't mean he can fly, bend bars of steel, or see through walls; it means simply that he can be happy and content in each and every circumstance. And the reason is that he has God.

How does he know? He knows it because, as he puts it elsewhere in the same letter, God came for him. God 'humbled himself' into the very depths of human experience in the person of Jesus Christ. This same Jesus died on a cross for him, enduring all the sin, the pride, envy, anger, gluttony, lust, greed and sloth of the world in that one point, not lashing out in revenge, but absorbing and neutralizing, forgiving it all. This same Jesus broke through death and rose again for him, giving him the promise that by placing his trust solely in him, one day he too would be raised after death to real, true, utterly complete life. As another biblical writer put it: 'This is how God showed his love among us: he sent his one and only Son into the world that we might live through him' (1 John 4:9).

There is nothing we can do to make God love us more than he does already. And there is nothing we can do to make God love us any less than he does already. God's love and compassion for us is not in any way dependent on our good fortune, job, status, achievement or looks. The starting point is not some huge effort to rid ourselves of sin; that can only be done once this first step has been taken, of grasping that God loved us before we ever thought of loving him, and that even our own sinful, compromised, half-hearted selves are loved and forgiven by God. So, says Paul, if we have God, whatever else we may or may not have, we have everything. And we don't need to envy anyone if we have what really matters.

There comes a point in the spiritual life when, having deposed ourselves from the highest place in our lives and priorities, we have to decide who takes that place. The secret of overcoming envy, of finding a true sense of worth, says Christian faith, is to make God the number one, the all-consuming passion of our lives: to pursue him, seek him, just as he has first pursued and sought us.

If the first step on the Christian road to goodness is to refuse to be a little god, the second step is to learn that we are loved and forgiven, and that we can be content with the person God has made us to be and is shaping in us. The next may be something altogether harder: to give over control and stop trying too hard; in short, to turn anger into peace.

4 Anger

On 2 October 2006, Charles Roberts, a 32-year-old truck driver, finished his night shift at 3 a.m. and went home for a brief rest. That night he wrote a note for his wife to read, looking back on the death of a premature daughter some years before. The note read:

I am filled with so much hate, hate toward myself, hate towards God and unimaginable emptiness.

It seems like every time we do something fun I think about how Elise wasn't here to share it with us and I go right back to anger.

In the morning, he dropped his children off at the school bus. He then took out an automatic pistol, walked the short distance to an Amish school in the small town of Paradise, Pennsylvania, entered a school building, shot five small girls dead and injured five more, before turning his gun on himself.

Anger can be deadly. It can undo a life in seconds, through the flash of a knife, or the pull on a trigger. It can mean years of fearful suffering under the threat of violence and rage. Our own anger may seem much less severe – more of the stubbed-toe or traffic-jam variety. Anger doesn't always end in the horrendous carnage that took place in Paradise that day (was ever a town more ironically named?), but this is the terminus, the final destination of the path down which anger leads.

Anger as a Solution

Yet anger is sometimes presented as a desirable, even an enviable thing in contemporary life. People who get angry often get their way, as the more timid of us tend to back down. So, in a society where getting what we want is pretty high up the list of targets, if anger is a good strategy for achieving that, then why not use it when it's to our advantage? If we think that it is always good to express oneself, rather than repressing feelings that rage inside, then we might think that allowing ourselves a good tantrum every now and again relieves the pressure and calms us down.

There's an element of truth to this. Anger is a useful human reaction. It is a valuable response to threat, enabling us to defend ourselves or others when under attack. It can be an appropriate response to cruelty or injustice or needless suffering. It can also fuel great passion and creativity. Martin Luther once said: 'When I am angry I can write, pray and preach well, for then my whole temperature is quickened, my understanding sharpened, and all mundane vexations and temptations depart.'

Luther's anger produced some fine works of passionate theological sense. It also at times fuelled bitter diatribes against his enemies which did nothing to promote the revolution in the church that he gave his life to. It's not hard to see how such anger quickly becomes the kind that causes yet more suffering, leaving a trail of regret and despair. Most psychological research now suggests that letting it rip actually tends to escalate irritation and makes a person likely to repeat the pattern even more frequently. Anger in the right place can be useful and even necessary. In the wrong place it can be fatal. Working out how to use it well is no easy task, precisely because strong emotions are involved, and it is hard to act wisely and thoughtfully when strong passions are flying around. Aristotle wrote: 'Anyone can become angry – that is easy. But to be angry with the right person, to the right degree, at the right time, for the right purpose, and in the right way – this is not easy.'

Charles Roberts' tragic story illustrates how anger often works. At the root of most destructive anger is pain. It starts with a feeling of having been cheated, abused or spurned. A lover is dumped, a friend is ignored, a child is neglected. It needn't be anything particularly substantial. Sometimes it can be as trivial as being cut up in a traffic jam, or not getting as much attention as we think we deserve. And then the process begins. The real or imagined slight is mulled over, dwelt on, thought about, turned over in the mind. As it grows, it is caressed, nurtured, fed and watered until it becomes all-consuming. At any stage along this process it might break out in violence or aggression at others, and they might not even have been the initial instigator of the offence at all. An angry person is a smouldering bonfire of resentment, ready to lash out at anyone who crosses their path, or who happens to remind them of the original cause of their hurt.

I recall once lounging around the garden of a student house I had just moved into with some friends when our elderly neighbour came down the back steps of his house, leant over the garden fence with a bright red face and started swearing blue murder at us at the top of his voice and trying to hit anyone within range with his walking stick. We were a bit bemused by this, to say the least, as we had hardly spoken to him at all yet. We tried to reason with him but there was no reasoning. In any case, if we got within a few feet of him we were likely to be rewarded with a sharp rap around the knees for our pains. We eventually retreated inside to avoid the torrent of abuse and the prospect of bodily harm. We asked some of the other neighbours, and worked out that around ten years ago some students had knocked down his garden wall and run away without paying up. Ever since then he had nursed his anger against anyone or anything that looked like a student. We simply served as a reminder of his grievance and were in the firing line. The same dynamic so often occurs in incidental and quite random murders. Someone who is deeply hurt, angry or lacking in self-regard at a vulnerable moment comes across someone who inadvertently triggers the same feelings of hatred, despair or fear that caused the pain in the first place, and the rest is fateful headlines.

Charles Roberts found he simply could not live with his festering wrath, and could only find respite through taking the lives of other children and ultimately killing himself. There was a twisted logic in his mind that day: if he could not enjoy his own child, then why shouldn't others know what he was feeling? Let someone else bear the pain for a while – and let his own pain cease by bringing an end to everything. Anger always has some small excuse, some nugget of truth that becomes the justification for mayhem.

The Symptoms of Anger

Psychologists describe anger as 'an emotional state that varies in intensity from mild irritation to intense fury and rage'. When we get angry, all kinds of physiological changes take place: our heart rates and blood pressure rise, as do our levels of energy-boosting hormones and adrenaline. Anger doesn't only show itself in loud, aggressive behaviour and throwing things around the room. There is such a thing as passive anger, when a person punishes the target of their anger by sulking, retreating into a corner or even making themselves physically ill. Yet whatever the personal effects, the social ones are devastating. Those who find themselves married to someone who cannot control their anger live in constant fear of the next outburst. To be at the receiving end of road rage is a frightening experience. To be shouted at in the street is distressing. Anger is no fun. It tends to generate either fear or yet more rage. Anger, like so many of the sins, usually hurts those who perpetrate it more than those who are the object of it. Seneca described it is 'an acid that can do more harm to the vessel in which it is stored than to anything on which it is poured'.

There are lots of anger management courses

around, offering all kinds of good advice about anger. They tend to focus on how to deal with feelings of anger and suggest habitual ways to deal with them when they arise. Advice ranges from breathing deeply to calm down, to repeating a relaxing word such as, well, 'relax' over and over, to visualizing a peaceful, calming scene such as a sunset or fishing by a gently flowing river. All of these can be very useful ways of dealing with anger that has become a regular habit, something that has a grip on us. Yet the Christian faith has some distinctive resources to offer here, some perspectives that help to make the fire of anger burn less fiercely in the soul.

Charles Roberts' tragic story gives us a hint of where Christian approaches begin. He was angry, first with himself and then with God. At the heart of his pain lay that deep distress at how things had turned out for him, and he blamed God. Thomas Merton once wrote: 'We are not at peace with others because we are not at peace with ourselves, and we are not at peace with ourselves because we are not at peace with God.' Roberts had at least recognized this; he just didn't know how to deal with that anger, that resentment towards God for dealing him such a cruel blow.

We saw in the last chapter how important it is to recognize that not everything that happens does so because God wills it. This insight becomes vital at this point as well. If God is the direct author of everything that happens, we might be entirely justified in getting angry at the way he arranges life. However, much of what happens in this life comes about as the result of sin and rebellion *against* God, or the chance events that happen when a world cuts itself off from the purposes of its creator, and it happens against his direct will. When this dawns on us and we stop blaming God for our misfortunes, it can open up the possibility that returning *to* God rather than turning *against* him holds the key to overcoming anger.

None of Your Business

Paradoxically, a Christian approach to dealing with anger begins with the notion of the anger of God. One of the starkest statements of the Bible is this: 'It is mine to avenge; I will repay' (Deuteronomy 32:35). It's one of the verses that reinforces the idea of the Old Testament God as a grumpy, wrathful deity, always looking to punish some passing victim who's enjoying themselves a bit too much. Along with the frequent ascriptions of vengeance to God, it seems to depict God as the perpetrator of anger, furious at most things. Yet divine anger is, when understood properly, a huge relief, and in fact the most priceless safeguard against destructive human anger to be found.

God gets angry at evil. That's the bottom line of divine wrath. In one of P. D. James' detective novels, *Original Sin*, two police officers discuss religion as follows:

'I don't go in for all this emphasis on sin, suffering and judgment. If I had a God I'd like him to be intelligent, cheerful and amusing.'

'I doubt whether you'd find him much of a comfort when they herded you into the gas chambers. You might prefer a God of vengeance.'

When we think about it, we wouldn't much like a God who didn't get angry at mass murder, pointless cruelty or cancer. A God who simply shrugged his shoulders, helpless or pathetically passive about such horrors, would be outrageous and certainly not worth worshipping. So in a sense we expect God to be angry sometimes. We just don't want him to be angry at us.

In the Bible, God is shown as getting angry when his people persistently suck up to wooden or stone idols 'just in case'. Such worship will diminish them. After all, if we worship something less than ourselves it tends to shrink us. Worshipping something or someone bigger than us – God for example – tends to enlarge and enrich us. God gets angry when the rich have no regard for the poor or even squeeze as much as they can from them. He gets angry when people misuse sex to abuse other people, especially women (see Amos 2:6–8, for example, for a good catalogue of the kinds of things that get up God's nose). The God depicted by the Bible is no shrinking violet, the calm, passionless figure found in some Eastern faiths. He is a God of fervent love and wrath, of compassion and fury.

In the New Testament, the apostle Paul takes that statement about God avenging and turns it into a powerful motivation for handling our own anger:

If it is possible, as far as it depends on you, live at peace with everyone. Do not take revenge, my friends, but leave room for God's wrath, for it is written: it is mine to avenge; I will repay, says the Lord. On the contrary: if your enemy is hungry, feed him; if he is thirsty, give him something to drink. In doing this, you will heap burning coals on his head.

ROMANS 12:18–20

If someone ignores me, treats me badly, cheats on me or lies shamelessly to me, and if God doesn't exist, then if I don't get back at them, no-one will. The injustice will lie smouldering in my heart and they will have got away with it, and so the most obvious way to deal with it is to get even with them, showing anger in either the sullen, passive form or the loud, violent version. If however there is a God whose job it is to deal with injustice and evil (as the God of the Bible is said to do), then that brings a whole new perspective to the situation. I can leave it to God to deal with them, either in this life or the next. It is a bit like a new kid in the playground who gets beaten up by a bigger kid in his class. He could try to get his revenge, but if he has an older brother higher up the school, then there's no point. He can relax and leave it to his bigger sibling to sort it out for him, restore order and make sure it doesn't happen again. Leave it to God to sort things out: that's his job, not mine. As William Willimon paradoxically puts it: 'Because God in Christ gets angry with us and the world, we don't have to. We can go on, delivered of the horribly dangerous terribly self-destructive sin of Anger.'

Paul advises his readers to handle anger in this way: as far as we possibly can, preserve peace between ourselves and anyone else. Of course there will be times where we need to resolve disputes, deal with tensions or protest against unfair treatment. Yet the advice here is, as far as possible, to keep anger out of it. Trying to solve problems through my own anger will probably cause more harm than good, as it will most likely lead to the other person feeling resentful in turn and wanting to get back at me in an ever-escalating cycle of bitterness.

Yet this bit of early Christian advice doesn't just stop there. Strong feelings are involved in anger, so rather than suppressing them, says Paul, go ahead and express them, but in a different and mischievous way. If you have to confront the person who has angered you, then go ahead, but do it in a way he or she least expects. Be really nice to them. Buy them a present.

Give them flowers. Go a step further than you normally would with anyone else; go out of your way to do them good. It's hugely counter-intuitive, and we can discern a sly smile playing around Paul's lips as he writes this, but we can begin to see what he's trying to do. Anger sometimes needs expressing, not repressing. Mark Twain's advice was: 'When angry, count four; when very angry, swear.' At least that's better than hitting someone! As we've seen, anger can be expressed in all kinds of different ways: actively, passively, violently or spitefully. Why not gracefully? If it's expressed that way, two things happen. One is that we 'heap burning coals on [our enemy's] head'. It doesn't sound a very pleasant or Christian image, but it simply means that he will be nonplussed, surprised, ashamed and baffled. If we want to get back at him, to get him to see the error of his ways, that route is much more likely to be successful than punching him in the face, or subjecting him to a torrent of foul-mouthed abuse.

The second thing that happens is that the cycle of violence is broken. Rather than an escalation of aggression, leading to more and more pain all round, graciousness and generosity are much more likely to draw the sting of the situation and replace it with harmony and peace. To bring the story of Charles Roberts full circle, his victims showed a remarkable ability to do as we have been learning. In the weeks after the deaths, not only did the Amish community forgive him, but they also set up a bank account to benefit the killer's family. The mother and grandmother of one of the small girls who was killed welcomed Roberts' own aunt into their home the day after the killing. This Christian community, viewed as a quaint relic of a long-gone age, showed a wisdom, maturity and virtue that far surpassed those of its supposedly more advanced neighbours. They had learnt how to turn anger into patience, forgiveness and love. It didn't bring back the five young lives that had been lost. But it did create something beautiful, some peace for tortured souls.

All this of course is rooted in a very profound and Christian insight into God. When we anger God, his first reaction is not in fact to punish at all. It is to forgive, to wait, to keep pouring down good things upon us. Jesus once said that '[God] causes his sun to rise on the evil and the good, and sends rain on the righteous and the unrighteous' (Matthew 5:45). In other words, even when people ignore him, use his name as a swear word, refuse to believe in him or treat his creation wastefully, he doesn't stop their supply of air, food and water to teach them a lesson. He goes on giving and giving. Of course there comes a point at which endless rebellion can't be allowed to succeed, but that is God's prerogative not ours, so we are to act like God in making that extra effort to 'bless those who curse you' and 'pray for those who persecute you'. One of the most beautiful and characteristic descriptions of God in the Old Testament is that he is 'a compassionate and gracious God, slow to anger, abounding in love and faithfulness' (Exodus 34:6, and lots of other places). If God is slow to get angry and quick to forgive, then maybe that's not a bad way for us to proceed.

Righteous Anger

Philosophers have argued for ages over whether anger can ever be justified, the Stoics for example arguing that it is always evil, and Aristotelians claiming that some anger can be good. Christians have tended to side with the Aristotelians on this, because they can conceive of one type of righteous anger: God's anger against evil. By extension, therefore, human anger against evil is also of value. A certain controlled passion against unnecessary hunger, suffering and injustice can be a powerful motivating force for active involvement in combating poverty or pain. A friend recently witnessed an argument between a man and a woman, presumably his wife or girlfriend. Hearing the abuse hurled at her caused a rising anger to grow in my friend, and when the argument turned violent that anger led him to step between them, defend the frightened woman and send the aggressor packing (it did help that my friend is 6 foot 5 and looks pretty scary). Such anger is a good and healthy thing. Anger is volatile and unstable, but it can lead to action. As Thomas Aquinas says, 'Anger, when it obeys judgments of reason, indeed disturbs reason to a degree, but it helps to promote readiness to execute the judgments.' Yet there is always a danger here. God might be able to sustain righteous anger for a long time (most of eternity, to be precise) but that's quite hard for us. Our righteous anger can quite quickly turn into a desire for vengeance. Anger that is not laced with love soon turns bad.

How do we know when anger slips from the righteous into the self-righteous? By definition it's hard to tell. If it were easier to tell, we'd all stop well before that stage. The Bible suggests that the best way of knowing is a matter of how long we allow ourselves to entertain it. The longer we let it lie, the more likely it is to turn bad on us. So deal with it quickly; it may be hard to let go of resentment, but not half as hard as in a year's time when it has begun to wrap its iron tendrils around our heart.

Don't Let it Settle

This is one the most characteristic pieces of Christian advice on anger: be ruthless with it before it takes deep root. In Jesus' manifesto sermon, put together by Matthew at the start of his Gospel, Jesus says something shocking to those of us who feel rather pleased with ourselves that we have never committed any *really* bad sin like murder:

You have heard that it was said to the people long ago, 'Do not murder, and anyone who murders will be subject to judgment.' But I tell you that anyone who is angry with his brother will be subject to judgment. Again, anyone who says to his brother, 'Raca,' [a juicy first-century Jewish insult] is answerable to the Sanhedrin. But anyone who says, 'You fool!' will be in danger of the fire of hell. Therefore, if you are offering your gift at the altar and there remember that your brother has something against you, leave your gift there in front of the altar. First go and be reconciled to your brother; then come and offer your gift. Settle matters quickly with your adversary who is taking you to court. Do it while you are still with him on the way, or he may hand you over to the judge, and the judge may hand you over to the officer, and you may be thrown into prison. I tell you the truth, you will not get out until you have paid the last penny.

MATTHEW 5:21–26

We might think murder is bad, but getting cross every now and again is OK. Jesus radicalizes the whole thing. Getting furious with a brother seems just as bad in Jesus' book. Why? Because the seed of murder always lies in unrestrained and unresolved anger, just as it did for Charles Roberts. So the advice of Jesus when we feel angry with someone is to go and sort it out quickly. Either sort it out in our own head, or if we have to, go and speak to the person who's angered us about it before it takes root in our soul.

One of the New Testament letters contains this nugget: 'In your anger do not sin: do not let the sun go down while you are still angry, and do not give the devil a foothold' (Ephesians 4:26–27). This contains a number of very honest and firm perspectives on anger. First there is the recognition that we will get angry, and that to feel anger is not in itself to do anything wrong. Guilt at feelings of anger is not a Christian response; anger in its place can be good and healthy, as we've already seen. On the other hand there is the realization that if anger is allowed to settle, it can give a beachhead for evil in a person's life; it 'gives the devil a foothold'. It is the tiny seed of resentment that, if left unchecked, can end up destroying everything in its path. If we allow bindweed to run unhindered in our garden and do nothing to uproot it, before long we will find it has strangled almost everything and is virtually impossible to get rid of. The only way to defeat it is to be ruthless: weed out every tiny bit of it in sight.

The same is true of anger. 'Don't let the sun go down while you are still angry' is a brilliant bit of practical advice. It's not a literal thing; sometimes angry feelings do take longer to heal, but the general idea is not to let anger grip us. Before we go to bed each night, we can think of anyone we feel angry with and forgive them. Turn that anger over to God: tell him it's his job to sort it out, to see that justice is done and that if something wrong has happened it gets its come-uppance.

Like most sins, anger takes something good – a proper hatred of evil and injustice – and twists it into something destructive: taking the law into our own hands and sustaining a long, smouldering campaign of vengeance. Anger is a dangerous thing for us humans. It deceives us into thinking that because we are in the right (and we may well be) our anger is justified, and if our anger is justified then we can express it how we like, or however it comes out. The heart of Christian wisdom on anger is that it is God's prerogative to exercise wrath. Although our anger can do some good, God alone can sustain righteous anger that will truly sort things out. Our anger tends to be fuelled by prejudice. 'Prejudice' comes from a Latin root – *pre-judice* – literally judging before the time, before we know the whole story. When we get angry and start to execute justice on our own behalf, we can only do so with a partial picture. We don't know why the other person cut us up in the car, lied to or deceived us, and whether they acted out of naivety, accident or malice. Only God knows the full story and that is why he alone is entitled to pass final judgments. All our judgments are penultimate not ultimate, tentative not conclusive. Of course at times we have to make judgments: when an employer writes someone a reference, a teacher writes a report or a judge or jury has to decide on guilt or innocence. Yet these judgments are to be made in a spirit of measured, level-headed clarity, not in the white-hot fury of anger. When we make judgments angrily, we are very likely to get them wrong, which is why we had better go easy on the anger. You and I had better learn to deal with our anger quickly, in the delicious relief of knowing that it's not up to us to sort the world out, but that God will one day do the job properly.

Anger and Silence

If there is a simple spiritual discipline that helps prevent destructive anger, it is the discipline of silence. Our anger is usually expressed in words: hateful, snarling, sharp words, often regretted very soon after they are uttered. The best remedy for this is to learn how to shut up. If anger is a regular problem, then the more we can learn just to remain silent and say nothing, the less likely we are to say things we might regret. Taking a short time every day to learn not to talk, to just be quiet and to let God do the gentle, quiet talking in our hearts helps us develop the ability to remain silent when we are under sore provocation to say something we'll soon regret. The apostle Peter writes of Jesus that 'when they hurled their insults at him, he did not retaliate; when he suffered, he made no threats. Instead he entrusted himself to him who judges justly' (1 Peter 2:23). Faced with the most appalling injustice of all time, Jesus was silent. Yet his silence did not signify acceptance or hopelessness. It was an eloquent way of expressing his trust in the God who does have the right to judge, whose job it is to sort out evil once and for all.

So far our journey has invited us to come down from our pedestals as little gods. It has visited the place where we can find forgiveness and be restored to a relationship with God. It has shown us how to give up control, to hand over the reins, to surrender. The next step on the road is to get our appetites in order so that we learn to desire what is good for us, not what will destroy us. It means managing our desires for food, sex and money so that they take their proper place in our lives. And that is what the next three chapters explore.

5 Gluttony

Why on earth is gluttony a sin? Most of us can see that pride is not very attractive, lust can get us into trouble, and envy is not a good feeling. But surely just eating a little too much is as harmless an activity as you can get? Other sins might damage other people – avarice might lead to theft and anger can end up in violence towards others – but surely gluttony harms no-one but yourself? Overeating on occasion is something most of us do on a night out, at Christmas or on a birthday; what can possibly be wrong with that?

One of the most famous gluttons in world literature, Shakespeare's Falstaff, makes the case for over-consumption, that to shun gluttony is to shun life:

If sack and sugar be a fault, God help the wicked. If to be old and merry be a sin, then many an old host that I know is damned: if to be fat is hated, then Pharaoh's lean kine are to be loved... Banish plump Jack, and banish all the world.

Strange though it may seem, in the earliest fourth-century lists of the deadly sins, gluttony used to head the list as the worst of them all. Pope Gregory wrote: 'Unless we first tame the enemy dwelling within us, namely our gluttonous appetite, we have not even stood up to engage in the spiritual combat.' Perhaps this was because those lists came out of the experience of the earliest monks, who had set their face against sins of luxury and bodily comfort, choosing instead a life of meagre physical comfort in exchange for the spiritual goods to be had instead. Gluttony stood for all the 'sins of the flesh' that they despised so much.

Later assessment of the rank of gluttony in the list has taken a kinder view. Thomas Aquinas was easier on gluttons because, like lust, overeating mainly concerns the body rather than the soul, and as we have to feed ourselves anyway, it is understandable and less serious than the other sins. In Dante's *Divine Comedy*, the poet arrives (in a dream) in purgatory, which he imagines as a mountain up which he climbs, hoping at the top to ascend even further into heaven itself. When he visits those who are still working off the effects of their sins in this life, he finds the gluttons in the third circle of upper hell, not far from the top, tantalizingly within sight of a succulent tree whose 'crop of tempting fruit ambrosial odours spread', but unable to climb up to taste them. For Dante, gluttons are certainly better than the prideful (firmly rooted to the foot of the mountain with a long way to climb), the envious, the wrathful, the slothful or the covetous. The only sin that seems less harmful to the poet is lust.

Dante has very good reasons for this, reasons that again might make us question why gluttony is considered a sin at all. Christianity actually likes food. Jesus, it seems, was rather fond of a party, regularly turned up at them, and mixed with people who also liked a good meal and a glass of wine or two. Many an abstemious, disapproving teetotal Christian has scratched their heads at Jesus' first choice of miracle (at least in John's Gospel): turning water into wine. Hence the common grumble from the religious people of Jesus' day that he was 'a glutton and a drunkard, a friend of tax collectors and sinners' (Matthew 11:19). Jesus was not especially choosy in the company he kept. This sentence was usually quoted to contrast Jesus with John the Baptist, a distant cousin, who took a more abstemious approach to life. He ate locusts and wore camel hair, and religious people accused him of being possessed by a demon. Jesus on the other hand seemed more 'normal', enjoying good food and drink, but he was accused of being a waster. You can't win with some.

As we shall see in more detail when we look at greed, Christianity is in one sense a very materialistic way of life. It celebrates physicality and the pleasures it can bring as God's good gift to us. Food is good because God made it. And presumably if he had just wanted us to be kept alive by food, rather than enjoy it as well, he would not have made so many varieties of it. A fine claret, a tasty slice of rich, creamy Camembert, a pint of dark beer, a sweet-tasting pear are all good, God-given pleasures. Thomas Aquinas sometimes seems to suggest that the sin in gluttony is enjoying food a bit too much. It is not the desire for food but indulgence in 'sumptuous food' that is sinful. Eating for the sake of keeping ourselves active is OK, but we're not meant to enjoy it. That doesn't quite seem to match the delight of the Psalmist, who celebrates 'wine that gladdens the heart of man, oil to make his face shine, and bread that sustains his heart' (Psalm 104:15).

Even more striking is that fact that the heart of Christian worship is not a solemn procession of priests or a drab litany of confession, but a meal. The only 'service' Jesus said was essential to Christian gatherings was eating together as a way of celebrating each other and remembering Jesus' life, death and resurrection, and in a way bringing them all into the present. If Christianity had it in for food, wine and enjoyment, it would be strange to make such an event the centre of our response to God and his gift to us.

What is Gluttony?

When we think of gluttony we normally think of very large people stuffing food into their mouths with no thought of tomorrow; over-indulgence to a huge degree. Yet the sin of gluttony has always been seen as covering a wider area than that, including that fastidiousness about food that obsesses over what we can and cannot eat. C. S. Lewis writes about the kind of old lady who simply asks for 'a cup of tea, weak but not too weak, the teeniest, weeniest bit of really crisp toast', adding, 'Because what she wants is smaller and less costly than what has been set before her, she never recognises as gluttony her determination to get what she wants, however troublesome it is to others.' Obsessive dieting can be just as much a sign of gluttony as overeating.

Gluttony then is an inordinate obsession with food, drink or plain consumption. It is getting food out of proportion, just as lust is getting sex out of proportion. The problem is that as we have seen in other chapters, our culture sends out some rather confused and mixed messages about consumption.

On the one hand we don't really consider gluttony a serious sin. A little over-indulgence is harmless and pleasant, and we feel generally it's fine to spoil ourselves a little from time to time. Yet in another sense, gluttony is the most hated and condemned sin of them all. Not because of what it might do to the soul, but because of what it can do to the body. Gluttony makes us fat, and that is the cardinal crime. Most sins we can hide: walking around city streets, we can't tell who regularly cheats on business deals, who is having an affair with their neighbour's husband, or who is full of overwhelming pride. But we can often tell those who have a habit of overeating by their size.

We have subtle ways of condemning such people. Just walk into any newsagent and look at the magazine section. Portrayed on almost every front cover are lithe, slim, tanned bodies (smooth for the women, muscular for the men), with not an ounce of fat in sight. Here are the ascetics of today, those who strenuously avoid the sin of gluttony and spend hours of penitential time in the gym, and they are rewarded for it with modelling contracts and the envy of all. As for those who have let themselves go a bit, each picture reinforces the sense that they fall short of the glory of man (or woman); they have failed in the quest for the perfect body, and it is all their fault. These very magazines are usually full of dieting tips or exercise routines to enable us to acquire the perfect body. The choice, we are told, is ours, and if we fail, there is no-one to blame but ourselves. There are few worse sins in a celebrity-obsessed culture than being fat.

Yet this view of the ugliness of fat is recent and culturally very relative. The semi-clad women who loll around in the seventeenth-century paintings of Rubens or Velasquez are far from the sylph-like, skin-and-bones models of the early twenty-first century. Their gentle rolls of white fat were considered beautiful then, and were signs of wealth and desirability. Thin bodies were considered a sign of poverty (clearly not having enough to eat), and bronzed skin was a sign of manual labour (having to work in the open air). The reasons we see thinness as beautiful and fatness as ugly are random, cultural and to be taken with a large pinch of salt.

We also have a real fascination with food. A TV advert lingers slowly over a picture of a chocolate sponge, soaked in brandy, with rich cream being poured over it, all with a soft, seductive voice-over describing the scene – a culinary striptease. The cookbook section of my local bookshop is far larger than the religious section. Who had ever heard of celebrity chefs thirty years ago? Now they are everywhere. The politics of food is also an area of tricky choices and legislation. Fine food and wine cost both time and money, and poorer families tend to eat less healthily. Should they be banned from doing so for their own good? Should we replace chips and hamburgers with healthy salads in school canteens despite what the kids want? When does the health of the nation override personal freedom to eat what we want?

Gluttony and Grace

The Bible does not, it's fair to say, have a lot to say about gluttony. Yet Jesus does give us one gem that helps point out the problem with an over-fascination with food. The Gospels tell the story of how Jesus was tempted by the devil early in his public career. It seems to have been an intense experience of spiritual trial, where Jesus' identity was at stake. Is he the Son of God? Will he obey God as a good son would, or is he an impostor, ready to chuck it in at the least excuse? Satan appears to him with the repeated refrain, 'If you are the Son of God, then prove it.' During the temptations, Jesus deliberately goes without food (we'll see why later). One of the enticements of the devil is to persuade Jesus to feed himself by the magic trick of turning the desert stones around him into bread. After all, that should be no problem to the Son of God, and it would of course demonstrate, by a display of miraculous power, his true identity. Jesus replies with a text from the Old Testament: 'It is written: "Man does not live on bread alone, but on every word that comes from the mouth of God."' (Matthew 4:4).

His point is that when food becomes a god, it becomes dangerous. Food, like sex, has the ability to skew things, and so it must be kept in its proper place. The evidence of that is all around. Obesity is one of the biggest (if you'll excuse the pun) problems in the developed world. Thirty thousand deaths are caused by obesity in Britain each year; 23 per cent of the population are obese and a further whopping 52 per cent are considered overweight. In the USA over 30 per cent are obese and a further 35 per cent are overweight. These figures would be cause for no more than a wry shake of the head were it not for the irony that they occur at a time when half the world, 3,000 million people, still lives on less than a dollar a day. Each year 1.7 million children still die from hunger-related diseases; that is one real child, someone's beloved son or daughter, somewhere in the world, every twenty seconds or so. By the time you finish reading this page another one or two will have gone. In 2006, for the first time, the number of overweight people in the world (1,000 million) overtook the number of malnourished people (800 million). First-world gluttony is scandalous when related to third-world poverty and hunger.

But overeating is not the only way of abusing food. Obsessing about quantities is also a sign of bad inner health. Bulimia and anorexia are not as common as obesity, but they still blight the lives of around 10 per cent of college-age girls in the USA, and in the UK two in every hundred school-age girls suffer from some kind of eating disorder. Anorexics reject food and hence reject life. Bulimics both accept and reject food, knowing they have real needs, but feeling they have to push those needs away. Compulsive eaters are typically needy for affection, people or stimulation. Some people veer between all three in a cycle of food-related distress. Suffering from anorexia, bulimia or a compulsive eating disorder are not sins as such, but they are an indicator that something is deeply wrong. Food is not a neutral thing, and in some complex way, our attitudes to food are all bound up with our spiritual and emotional health.

This begins to reveal to us the reasons why Christianity has found gluttony to be a sin, and again it comes back to the biblical picture of human beings as whole people, whose emotional, physical and spiritual needs are all bound up together, and one part affects the others. It also points back again to the Christian conviction that at the heart of all our ill-health, our self-harm and the damage we do to each other and to the planet on which we live lies our connection, or lack thereof, to the God who made us.

Why do people overeat themselves into obesity, or starve themselves into anorexia? All the studies suggest that these disorders often emerge from a sense of lack of worth. We all know the pattern of comfort eating. When we feel a bit low, a slice of chocolate cake or apple pie can make us feel a whole lot better. Ten pints of lager or a couple of stiff whiskies can help us forget why we felt bad in the first place. Similarly, anorexia or bulimia often emerge out of patterns of unhappiness or self-dislike. The Eating Disorder Association says that such patterns of self-abuse are usually caused by such things as 'low self-esteem, family relationships, problems with friends, the death of someone special, problems at work, college or at university, lack of confidence, sexual or emotional abuse. Many people talk about simply feeling "too fat" or "not good enough".'

Now these of course are extreme cases. Yet they

point to the ease with which we use food and drink to replace something that's missing from our lives, to comfort us when we feel lonely and to satisfy us when we are not just physically, but also spiritually hungry.

Peter Kreeft, an American philosopher and writer, puts it well: 'The motivation for gluttony is the unconscious self-image of emptiness: I must fill myself because I am empty, ghostlike, worthless.' Gluttony is trying to fill a spiritual vacuum with a physical remedy. It is like taking penicillin for a broken heart. There's nothing wrong with penicillin, but it doesn't do much good for a restless soul, and too much of it can lead to all kinds of problems.

Recognizing and Reacting to Gluttony

So how do we know when we are in danger of gluttony? The guilt feelings that come when we know we have eaten too much once in a while, or indulged in a particularly creamy slice of cheesecake, are most probably not true, healthy signs of guilt; they are probably just a tinge of regret that these indulgences take us further from the lithe body we wish we had – once on the lips, forever on the hips. A moment's pleasure for the palate means an hour's pain with the pedometer. That's not a moral issue, and it may be caused more by vanity than gluttony.

Gluttony happens when the connection between

food and its proper purpose is broken. Food is given to sustain the body, to enrich our communal life and to give pleasure to the taste. It is not there to comfort the isolated and lonely, to bolster a fragile self-image or to be a substitute for prayer. If we begin to recognize that we are regularly eating alone for spurious reasons, for reasons that seem different from the purpose of food itself, that may be when we need to watch out for the place of food in our life, or to get some help.

Gluttony rears its head when someone begins to get food out of proportion. The key issue here is control. The overeater loses control over how much he eats. He is unable to stop himself taking the extra-large Coke, the extra cream on the pudding, to finish off the packet of biscuits rather than stop at one. He believes the lie that it is impossible for him to control his eating. For the anorexic or bulimic person, the issue is the other way round: it is a matter of giving up control. For many who sufferer from such diseases, or those who might have a tendency in that direction, the problem is too tight a control over what they eat, and their very identity becomes bound up with their illness. Here, the remedy is to learn to give up control and re-form their identity around something other than eating habits, so that food can take its normal place as something to be enjoyed.

Neither anorexia nor bulimia are sins in themselves. They are patterns of destructive behaviour that often afflict people for deeper reasons than we can fathom. However, as we've seen before, sin is a complex, tangled, murky thing, where choices we make intertwine with powers over which we have little control to leave us stuck in patterns of behaviour that are literally self-destructive. Eating disorders are an extreme version of what can happen when food gets out of proportion, and when it begins to usurp the place of God in a person's life.

Speaking of the emptiness that gluttony tries to fill with food, Peter Kreeft goes on to give the Christian answer to that emptiness: 'Only a knowledge of God's love for me can fill that emptiness, make me a solid self, give me ultimate worth.' If the abuse of food often comes from a deep sense of dis-ease, a loss of self-worth, then the Christian answer to finding a true sense of being worth something is that it can come only from the God who made us. Only when our desperate search for love is met by the deepest and most satisfying love of all, the love of a God who is Love, do these deepest hurts begin to be healed. In his novel *The Good Soldier* Ford Madox Ford wrote: 'We are all so afraid, we are all so alone, we all so need from the outside the assurance of our own worthiness to exist.' We keep on trying to create that (re)assurance through romance, sex or food, yet it can only truly come from 'outside' – not just outside ourselves, but outside this world – from the God who made it and us. Gluttony is disordered desire. It is thinking that food can satisfy our deepest needs. And no created thing can do that. We were made to find our deepest satisfaction when we are connected with our creator; when we learn to desire him above everything else.

Of course, recovering from such behaviour patterns can take a long time, as it does with most sins. Yet the crucial first step is to hand over control. Alcoholics Anonymous have understood this for years. The centre of their twelve-step programme, which has its roots deep in Christian therapy, is the act of recognizing that consumption of alcohol has got out of control. Only help from outside can break the cycle and enable us to 'make a decision to turn our will and our lives over to the care of God as we understand him'. And it works. Since it was founded in 1935, two million people have claimed that the AA approach has helped them manage their alcoholism.

Whether the issue is overeating or undereating, the Christian answer is to hand over control. Not just some of it, all of it. We do not have to binge on food or restrict it to the tiniest portion. We do not have to let food dominate our lives; it was never meant to. But that can only happen through a conscious act of giving up control to God, who alone can help break the patterns of self-abuse. That way, a new identity can be formed. No longer is food the defining factor in a person's self-image. Instead they are essentially someone who is loved and welcomed by the God who came into human life in the person of Jesus Christ. This step of handing over control is not easy, but it is the only way: finding a sense of self-worth and value through the one true God who made us and loved us.

Alcoholics Anonymous talks of this as a 'higher power'. Yet Christianity goes a step further by giving this higher power a name. We are not asked to hand over control to a nameless, faceless god, who might for all we know be indifferent or even malign. We are asked to hand over power to a God of deep, passionate love, a God who has himself experienced hunger, tears, pain and forsakenness and overcome them all. We are asked to hand over control to the God of Jesus Christ. A friend of mine grew up with an alcoholic mother, and describes living in a home dominated by over-consumption: 'I was learning to live with chaos and uncertainty… I felt unloved and worthless so what I did was to look to other things to try to fill that hole and make me feel valuable and loved.' Not surprisingly he turned to alcohol, reckless spending and meaningless relationships and was heading down the same path as his mother. He turned to AA, and found the twelve-step programme hugely beneficial, yet still lacking something: 'I realized that just believing in a higher power wasn't enough. There was still something gnawing inside me.' Then he stumbled on a warm, friendly church and attended an Alpha Course: 'I found something which I had been looking for all my life. It was as if the "God-shaped hole" in me was being filled... What had been missing in my life was any understanding of the life of Jesus and the love of God. That was the final piece of the jigsaw. I had known about the higher power, but nothing about Jesus.'

Healing Gluttony

What then is the Christian answer to gluttony? Simple: it is not dieting, but fasting. Or more exactly, the age-old rhythm of fasting and feasting. For as long as the Christian church has been around, fasting and feasting have formed part of the normal disciplines of the Christian life. The Christian year consists of periods of normal consumption, punctuated by times of fasting (to remind us that food needs to be kept in its place) and feasting (to remind us that food is a very good thing). The feasts of Easter and Christmas are preceded by the fasts of Lent and Advent. In between, there is just normality.

On the whole, Christians have tended to be careful about making fasting compulsory, preferring to recommend it as a useful discipline from time to time. Fasting serves as a means of keeping food in its proper place, ensuring that we retain control of our appetites rather than being controlled by them. Christians do not fast because food is a necessary evil, as if the ideal state for human beings were not to eat at all. On the contrary, there is far more in the Bible about feasting than fasting. However, the practice of regularly denying ourselves food, or a particular kind of food for a temporary period such as Lent, is a way of keeping control, of reminding ourselves that food is good to liven up an evening with friends, to keep our body and mind functioning properly and to delight our taste buds, but it is not the be-all and end-all of life. It is also a reminder that to lose control of our desire for food is to threaten not only our physical size, shape and functionality, but also our heart and soul. Gluttony doesn't just damage the body, it also harms the spirit.

Fasting can also connect us more closely to the hungry. If one of the scandals of our age is a world of obesity right next door to millions who are starving, then the experience of going without food every now and again can increase our sense of solidarity with those whose frequent experience is famine. It is hard to feel for the starving if the least twinge of an empty stomach is always satisfied with a ready-to-hand biscuit or piece of cake. There is nothing like feeling real pangs of hunger to help you identify with, begin to understand and perhaps even do something about the suffering of the hungry in this world.

Fasting serves to restore equilibrium to a human life. I have a barometer in my hallway at home. To enable it to show the current air pressure and predict the weather, I have to tap it or shake it every now and again to bring it back to its proper place. Fasting is a way of tapping our spiritual barometer. Christians usually combine fasting with prayer, and a time of paying special attention to God and what he might want to speak quietly into their hearts and minds. Abstaining from food is a way of making the point to ourselves and to God, and to anyone else for that matter, that we do not choose to live 'by bread alone, but by every word that proceeds from the mouth of God'.

But fasting is to be complemented by feasting. Feasting stops us from finding our identity or worth in our ability to deny ourselves, or in our self-control. It encourages us to enjoy food and drink thankfully. It stops short of bingeing, getting drunk and losing total control so that we end up doing all kinds of things we later regret, but it does tell us to have a little fun!

Fasts are preliminary to feasts. Both remind us that food is not everything; fasts by denying over-indulgence, and feasts by focusing on the event being celebrated – the coming of Christ, God himself, in human from at Christmas, or the triumph over death at Easter. Even in Christian feasts, food is a means to an end: a means of celebrating something of ultimate value and worth.

The Christian answer to gluttony is not self-denial for the sake of it, nor is it the boring routine of endless moderation, a meagre diet of lettuce leaves and dry bread. It is the rhythm of feasting and fasting, the ability to take time to enjoy the delicious flavour of a Belgian chocolate, an Italian ice cream or some English strawberries when the time is right, yet to say no to any of these at other times, because our deepest needs are not met by food, but by fellowship with God.

6 Lust

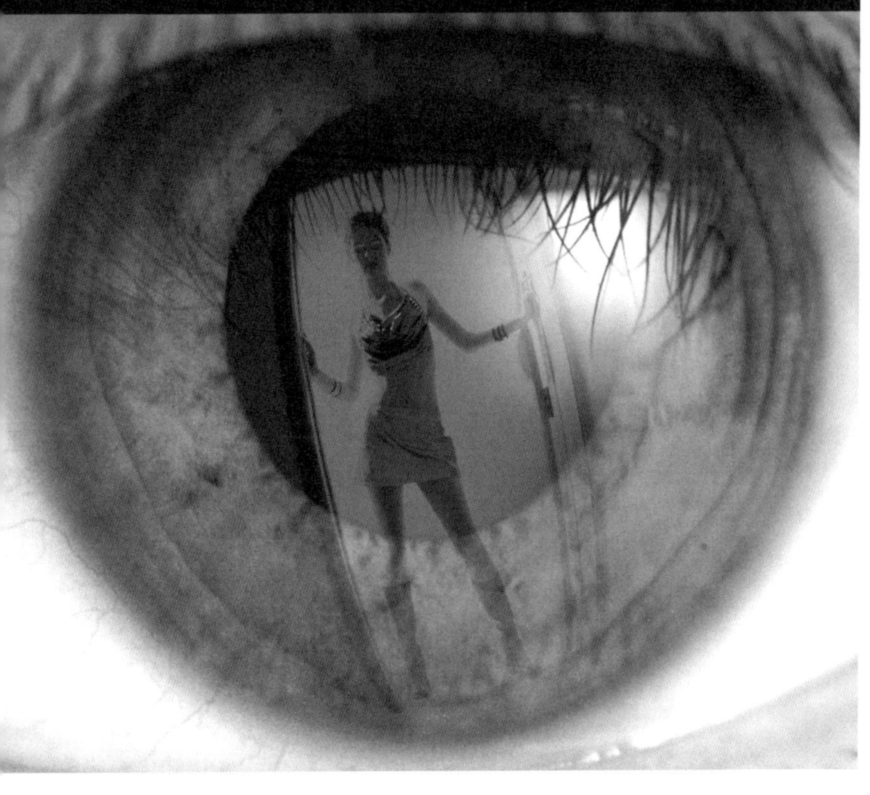

We tend to think that lust hardly needs definition. Our world has such a fascination with it that we think we know only too well what it is and what it feels like. However, there is one important point to be made at the outset. Lust is not the same as sexual desire. Of course the church has a bit of a chequered history on this, but by and large Christians have always believed that sexual desire is a good and healthy thing, given by God and to be celebrated. After all, there is a whole book of the Bible dedicated to it – the Song of Solomon, one of the most sensual and erotic love poems in world literature. If the Bible had it in for sex, it's hard to see how such a book would have got past the censors.

As we've seen with just about all the sins so far, evil is not very creative. It just takes something good and twists it, distorting it into something destructive and painful. As should be patently clear by now (at the risk of repeating myself) the physical pleasure of sex is a good, healthy and positive thing. Sexual feelings are God's gift to us and it would be unnatural and odd not to experience them at all. Christian hostility to lust is not hostility to sex.

Make no mistake; for all our jokes about sex, unbridled lust is deadly. If lust really takes hold of a person it will destroy everything: their mind, their closest relationships, their reputation and even their body. It can lead to broken marriages, shame, endless regret and, most destructive of all, child abuse or rape. Chaste people are not immune from catching HIV, but they are less likely to do so. So, if sex is fine but lust is not, wherein lies the difference? What is so wrong with lust?

Lust happens when sexual attraction becomes the dominant and overpowering factor in the relationship between two people. It happens when all a person can think about when they look at someone else is their body, and what it would be like to take it, possess it, conquer it. It can happen in married relationships as well as unmarried ones. Thomas Aquinas likens it to a lion who, seeing a stag, thinks of nothing else but the meal it is about to enjoy: fun for the lion, but not good news for the stag. Lust, like gluttony, is disordered desire. Just as gluttony gets our desire for food out of proportion, so lust gets our desire for sex out of proportion.

The desire of lust is for conquest and possession. It is also about personal, physical satisfaction. It thinks of the other person as a means of getting that satisfaction, of releasing the tension of sexual desire. And as such it makes the other person less than a person. They become just the means through which a physical need can be satisfied or relieved; a bit like a hamburger or even a toilet. Generally speaking, most people I know don't like being treated as if they were a bag of chips or a public convenience. Some people might enjoy being the object of lust, because it indicates sexual attractiveness and the power over others that it brings. It is less fun when the attentions are unwanted.

This is what lies at the heart of lust: pure selfishness. And that is its problem. Thomas Aquinas says it simply: 'We designate sexual lust self-love.' In the Bible, the classic example of the destructiveness of lust comes in a story about King David, one of the great heroes of the Bible, yet deeply flawed when it came to this area of life. Looking out over his city one day, he spies a beautiful woman named Bathsheba bathing on the roof of her house. He wants her, will do anything to get her and, being a king, gets his way. She becomes pregnant and covering it up means arranging for the murder of her husband. The ugly deed is done, bringing untold sorrow and tragedy into their lives, and leading indirectly to the break-up of David's kingdom. It all comes from lust, David's self-centred obsession with possessing and conquering Bathsheba for himself (the story is found in 2 Samuel 11–12, and David's poem of deep remorse comes in Psalm 51).

Lust happens when one person treats another person as just a body and no more; as an instrument, a means to an end, not an end in themselves. Lust is bad, not because sex is 'dirty', but because sexual desire distorted in this way is deeply and cruelly self-centred. And this is also at the heart of the difference between sex and lust: with good sex, we aim first and foremost to give, and we end up receiving as well. With lust the primary motive is to get, and although there may be some temporary relief, the end result is just more frustration.

The Elizabethan poets especially understood this. In one of his early poems, John Donne depicts a careless lover, seeing his conquest as no more than a tasty morsel:

And when hee hath the kernel eate
Who doth not fling away the shell?

If the primary aim is the relief of tension, the pride of conquest or the satisfaction of desire, then as soon as that has been achieved, distaste usually sets in and the means through which the goal has been achieved is discarded. One of Shakespeare's sonnets captures the violent and unpredictable nature of lust, leading to disdain of the 'beloved':

Th'expense of spirit in a waste of shame
Is lust in action, and till action, lust
Is perjur'd, murd'rous, bloody, full of blame,
Savage, extreme, rude, cruel, not to trust,
Enjoyed no sooner but despised straight,
Past reason hunted, and no sooner had
Past reason hated as a swallowed bait,
On purpose laid to make the taker mad.

When we are dealing with lust rather than love, the person involved is just a vehicle, an instrument, a thing to satisfy desires. That is why lust is fundamentally selfish and why lust is bad for a person: because it fosters the illusion that he or she is at the centre of the universe.

It doesn't take much imagination to see how lust destroys its objects: the beaten wife, the abused child, the victim of the sexual predator. But it also destroys the person who indulges it too. Lust destroys relationships and marriages. If one partner feels treated like a slab of meat by the other, just there for the sex, it is a classic recipe for a break-up on the horizon. Many crimes of rape are committed out of lust, and these acts not only destroy the lives of their victims but of their perpetrators as well.

Lust in the Modern World

Like so many of the other sins, lust has become truly rehabilitated in our culture. Invitations to lust are everywhere. Lithe, toned bodies, both male and female, pose seductively on magazine covers, the sides of buses and late-night TV. A random visitor from another planet would be forgiven for concluding that sex and the stimulation of sexual desire was for us the highest good, the greatest goal, the most sacred centre of life. It seems we live in a society that exalts 'the lust of the eyes' (1 John 2:16) as the most central, urgent and primeval urge, the pinnacle of human existence.

Yet in fact the reality is much more complex than that. Although on the one hand our culture is fascinated by sex, at a deeper level we live in a world that trivializes it. Allan Bloom captures this in his book *The Closing of the American Mind*. He recalls a conversation in which a student wondered what all the fuss was about. His words were: 'Sex? It's no big deal.' His point was that sex was just normal, ordinary; why make such a big issue of it? Many people find the traditional Christian teaching, that sex should be kept for marriage, strange to say the least. Another student said: 'Sex has been part of my life since I was sixteen. If I'm going out with someone and I love them, why shouldn't I have sex with them? It doesn't harm anyone else: it's our business anyway.' For her, Christian restraint on sexual behaviour was irrelevant (everyone does it), unrealistic (do you really expect me to control my desires?) and outdated (contraception has changed all that).

The assumption underlying this trivialization of sex is that sexual desire is just another physical function, like eating, drinking or relieving oneself. The next stage in the argument is that we should therefore treat sex just like eating, drinking and relieving ourselves, so we are free to do it whenever we feel like it. It seems a straightforward argument. However, it's one that begins to fall apart when we look at it more closely.

Sex is not like eating or drinking. For a start, we all need to eat and drink to stay alive, but despite what our culture sometimes implies, it is quite possible to live without sex, and even to lead a life that is content and fulfilled. After all, Jesus did. The other obvious difference of course is that sex involves another person. When it is treated as only a physical act, it is reduced from the mysterious, ecstatic union of two created beings who are bound together inextricably in a lifelong, passionate bond to a matter of mechanics. In other words, when sex is reduced to lust, it gets trivialized, becomes boring and turns into just a bodily function, like an animal looking for prey.

When this happens, sex gets commodified, separated from the difficult and complicated business of real relationships and real people. In the film *Indecent Proposal* a young couple, as deeply in debt as they are in love, are tempted by an invitation from a millionaire for the woman to spend a night with him in exchange for a million dollars. As the young couple debate what to do, they decide to take up the offer, with Demi Moore's character uttering (rather unconvincingly) the clinching line: 'It's only my body. It's not my soul.'

If only it were that simple. The woman goes ahead, spends the night with the millionaire, and returns to her fiancé. Yet the night has ruined everything. It brings distrust, pain, tension and eventually leads to the break-up of the relationship. It was not quite so easy to disentangle body and soul as the couple had imagined. The problem is, again, trivialization. They thought sex with someone else was fine because it only involved a bodily activity; it didn't affect the rest of their lives. But the truth is that we can't compartmentalize ourselves in that way. What we do with our bodies affects our souls, our hearts and our minds.

The myth that sex is just like food and drink – the satisfaction of a purely physical need – is pervasive and deeply wrong. To have sex with someone is to enact the most intimate of human relations; it is to touch them at the deepest level of their being. It is not so much picking an apple off a tree as disturbing the roots. Societies tend to develop taboos, a certain embarrassment or caginess about areas where they know themselves to be vulnerable and easily hurt. So it's not surprising that many societies place taboos around such topics as death and sex. Why? Because we know we are at risk at precisely these points, and we need to tread with immense care. We are on holy ground.

Satisfying Lust?

But this is the wisdom of the ages. It is not the wisdom of today, with the current explosion in the availability of opportunities to luxuriate in lust. It is now not just a matter of middle-aged men in raincoats sitting in dingy strip clubs or smelly cinemas; it is internet porn just a few clicks away at any time, or adult channels on satellite or hotel TVs, just waiting to be accessed. Pornography lives on a rhythm of secrecy, silence and shame, until the point comes where shame is no longer felt.

The argument for such wide availability of porn is of course the freedom to choose. There is always the 'off' button. No-one is forced to watch, and those who want to should be free to do so. The difficulty with this argument is that it assumes we are perfectly balanced people, quite coolly capable of choosing for ourselves what is good for us or for society, with no competing factors getting in the way. But that is far from the case. The Christian understanding of the human will is that we are not as free to choose as we might think. We easily become addicted to different forms of sin. For some, their relationship to lust is more like that of a heroin addict to his drug than someone choosing between orange and apple juice for breakfast. We might invite a recovering alcoholic to stay at our home and put him in a bedroom with a well-stocked drinks cabinet, but it's probably not a good idea. Non-alcoholics would be fine, but those with a weakness in this area had better steer clear, or better still, be protected from such an invitation to self-destruction. Sexual desire is a potent force that can make us do all kinds of things against our better judgment. What if this is a real area of vulnerability that we mess around with at our peril? If a person is weak and vulnerable in this area of their life, why on earth need they be drawn into the seedy world of porn, which will only damage them and others?

Pornography is of course a multi-million-pound industry. And where money is involved, we are wise to take with a pinch of salt the arguments that justify those who make money out of us. So often the appeal to 'freedom of choice' is exactly that: a barely concealed justification for the vast profits made by porn barons out of human misery.

The other argument for the use of porn, often assumed rather than articulated, is that pornography allows for the harmless release of sexual tension. Just a quick burst of porn, masturbation or sexual activity gets it out of the system, again using the old, mistaken analogy that our desire for sex is like our desire for food. If you feel hungry, have a sandwich: it will make you feel better. The problem is that lust is like eczema. The more we scratch it, the more it itches. Stimulation does not lessen sexual desire and tension. It may give temporary relief, but in the long term it just increases it. As the American writer Frederick Buechner puts it: 'Lust is the craving for salt of a man who is dying of thirst.' If someone fills their mind with images that are bound to provoke lust, then those are the images that will spring up in their mind in idle moments. Lust is a cruel master; it never lets go easily once it has got its teeth into a person. Even the notorious Marquis de Sade knew this from the inside: 'Lust's passion will be served; it demands, it militates, it tyrannizes.' His answer was to give in to it, to give himself up to its clutches. This might not be the best advice, though…

So what does Christianity have to say about lust? Perhaps in the past some people thought lust was the worst sin because it promised them the most pleasure, but that isn't a Christian way of thinking. Sometimes we can think that just because something is enjoyable it must be bad, but a God who created pleasure for us would hardly think that way. Christians have traditionally thought pride to be much worse than lust. As Peter Kreeft says of lust: 'It may be the widest road, but it is not the deepest pit.' Thomas Aquinas notes how Christians are prone to get a bit too interested in condemning sexual sin as if it were the worst of all. Sexual sin is no worse than any other, but it is still highly destructive.

Time and again the writers of the Bible warn against letting lust get its grip on us. Jesus himself was uncompromising on it:

'You have heard that it was said, "Do not commit adultery." But I tell you that anyone who looks at a woman lustfully has already committed adultery with her in his heart. If your right eye causes you to sin, gouge it out and throw it away. It is better for you to lose one part of your body than for your whole body to be thrown into hell.'

MATTHEW 5:27–29

Strong stuff. No doubt Jesus was exaggerating to make a point in the way that rabbis would sometimes do, but even so this is a pretty stiff warning against venturing merrily down the seductive path of lust.

What does he mean by 'looking lustfully'? A child does not always know the difference between hunger and greed, but there is one. In the same way, there is a difference between proper sexual attraction and lust, and that difference needs to be learnt. It was once said that the difference between looking and looking lustfully is about five seconds. There is a difference between admiring beauty in someone else and lingering over that beauty and allowing it to grow into the desire to possess and invade it. Jesus' dramatic words point out the source of all lust – our own hearts and desires – and advises us to learn how to nip it in the bud before its twirling, sticky tendrils wrap themselves firmly around our souls.

Bodies and Souls

Some religions (and to be honest, some forms of Christianity in the past) have thought of human beings primarily as souls entrapped in rather unfortunate and temporary prisons called bodies. They say that our souls are not really meant to be tied down by flesh, and their destiny is to be released from our bodies, to soar to a spiritual realm above this lesser physical one. Other religions or worldviews tend in the other direction: that we are primarily bodies with physical needs and the spirit is left to one side.

Christian theology has always insisted that we are both body and soul, and that the two are inextricably entwined – so much so that we cannot separate them. Christianity understands human beings as fully fused, integrally related beings, made up of a physical and spiritual nature, which might be conceivable as separate entities in theory, but cannot be distinguished in practice. We are both physical and spiritual.

Any Christian who has understood this therefore cannot treat people as if they are just bodies, or just souls. Sometimes it has been suggested that the only really important bit about people is their souls or spirits, so that it doesn't matter whether they experience hunger or injustice or pain as long as their spirits are pure and holy. Lust goes the other way, treating other people as if they were just bodies and nothing else. Both get it wrong, because we are neither souls nor bodies, but both.

Lust simply misreads people. It misunderstands them, demeans them, reduces them. Because we cannot separate our spiritual from our physical natures, sex is a profoundly spiritual as well as a physical act. It touches us at the deepest levels, both body and soul. Lust clumsily tries to do the first without doing the second, and it just isn't possible.

The traditional Christian teaching that sex has to be held within strict limits, the limits set by the lifelong commitment of marriage, is held for exactly this same reason. If we are spiritual animals, with souls, minds, hearts and bodies all entwined with each other, then to have the most intimate physical union of bodies without a corresponding spiritual union of heart, minds and, most importantly, lives, is to live a lie. It is to pretend that we are serious about wanting someone else when we only really want part of them. A friend once entitled a talk about extra-marital sex 'Lying in Bed', and he was exactly right.

A halfway house is to say that of course promiscuous behaviour is out of order, but if one person loves another, then surely they do have a union of hearts and minds. Surely a mere piece of paper adds nothing more? If we love someone, why not go to bed with them? But that begs a whole set of other questions. How do we know whether we love someone? Is it feeling a certain way about them? Fancying them? What happens if we lose those feelings next year or next week, or when we wake up next to them in the morning? The novelist Julian Barnes writes of how careful we need to be with those easily abused words.

I love you. For a start we'd better put these words on a high shelf; in a square box behind glass which we have to break with our elbows; in the bank. We shouldn't leave them lying around the house like a tube of Vitamin C. If the words come too easily to hand, we'll use them without thought… we'll get drunk or lonely or… plain damn hopeful and there are the words gone, used up, grubbied.

The words 'I love you' are very special words; we ought to use them with care. True love means valuing someone enough to give ourselves unreservedly to them, loving them enough to stick with them, not just when things go well or for whatever we can get out of them, but when things turn bad and the relationship becomes for a while more about giving than receiving. What if they suddenly became bankrupt or sick or disabled? Do we love them enough to stick with them then? And how do we know if we're really willing to do that? True, committed, faithful love involves making a commitment to another person. Making it public helps: openly promising in front of the people we know and whoever else wants to listen, so there's no room for doubt, that we give ourselves to another person, for better, for worse, for richer, for poorer, in sickness and in health. Marriage is much more than a piece of paper. The piece of paper (or perhaps better, the gold ring) serves as proof, evidence for the whole world to see, of the exclusive commitment that lies at the heart of true love.

If we love someone like that, we should go right ahead and enjoy the best sex we can, giving and receiving without an ounce of guilt or remorse. That is the true union of souls and bodies, hearts and lives. If not, then it might be wiser to go easy on the words 'I love you', and it might be more honest to hold back from the sex as well.

Now that sounds hard, almost impossible in our over-sexualized culture. This is one of the areas in which Christian moral teaching runs right across most contemporary codes. Yet it explains the reason for the Christian awareness of the sacredness of sex and why Christians have always wanted to handle it with care. How can such a life be lived in such a heavily sexualized culture, especially for single people? The easiest place to live this life is in a community where sex is not a constant topic of conversation, where every little innuendo doesn't get made into a snigger, and where there is true intimacy and friendship, along with a clearly agreed rule that good, deep friendships between people of the opposite sex don't have to end up in bed. In other words, a community that manages to be what a church is meant to be: a group of people who are fully aware of their own weaknesses and vulnerabilities, yet who have decided to try to walk this path of Christian life together and to help each other enjoy real freedom from the destructiveness of lust. Lust can be overcome and replaced by healthy, rounded, strong relationships, but only if we begin to learn to relate to each other as whole people, more than just bodies, people worthy of respect because they are made in God's image, body and soul, full and complete.

Christianity celebrates sex in the context of marriage. It teaches people to guard marriage relationships with the utmost care (and hence to be careful about not developing too intimate relationships with those outside the marriage). For those who are single, Christianity promotes another wonderful expression of human sexuality: celibacy. Many think of celibacy as a negative thing – just the absence of sex. In the Bible and in Christian history, however, celibacy has always been prized as a precious and positive way of life. It leaves time and energy for all kinds of other priorities and relationships, and in particular for a special devotion to God and his wider purposes in the world. As the apostle Paul puts it: 'I would like you to be free from concern. An unmarried man is concerned about the Lord's affairs – how he can please the Lord. But a married man is concerned about the affairs of this world – how he can please his wife – and his interests are divided' (1 Corinthians 7:32–33). Many people who have chosen the path of celibacy have been freed to give themselves to the poor and deprived, in a way that is almost impossible for those with a wife or husband and children, Mother Teresa being a classic example.

Overcoming Lust

How then is lust overcome? One big mistake is to try to eliminate sexual desire altogether. Unfortunately, Christian theologians in the past from Jerome onwards have sometimes portrayed sex as unclean and unhealthy, requiring cold showers and hair-shirts. Such desire was depicted as disturbing the tranquil repose of the ideally balanced soul. The aim was somehow to remove desire, leaving the human soul an oasis of peaceful, untroubled calm. These methods don't tend to work for one simple reason: they mistake sexual feelings for lust. Sexual feelings are part of being human and cannot be entirely eliminated, nor should they be.

The first place where lust is healed is in relationship to God. It is when we come back to God and learn to see other people as God sees them that it is possible to begin to overcome lust within the heart. If we find ourselves looking at someone else lustfully, we can try to see them as God sees them: living a whole human life with parents, friends, brothers or sisters, in a job or at home, with needs, struggles and weaknesses, just like everyone else. In other words, we can put them in context and bring them to mind as full, rounded people. We might just find that we begin to develop a richer, more complete view of them, and the sexual attraction, while maybe not removed, will find its proper place. As we do this we find we are learning to see them as a whole person, as part of a wider network of relationships, in a family, in space and time, in friendships.

Another approach is to think ahead. In Homer's *Odyssey*, the goddess Circe warns the traveller Odysseus about the seductive voices of the Sirens, and how their beautiful voices will inevitably lure him and his crew to their deaths. Odysseus' inquisitive nature is torn between desire to hear the sound, and fear of where it will lead him. So, knowing his own weakness and desire, and following Circe's instructions, he has himself tied to the mast, so that when he hears the Sirens' alluring voices he will not be tempted to follow them to his destruction. He also ensures his crew's ears are filled with wax so they will hear neither the voices of the sirens nor his own cries to be untied to follow them. Odysseus should never have sailed that close to the Sirens anyway, but nevertheless this story contains quite a bit of wisdom. If we know we are going to be tempted by something that will cause us trouble, and we doubt whether we can resist, we can think ahead and put in place things that will restrain us when the time comes.

We have already noted the importance of walking this path together, being part of a community that isn't saturated with innuendo and suggestive images. Some people who have started to walk the Christian path, and who have struggled with lust, ask friends to help. This can mean finding a couple of close friends of the same gender who understand where we are coming from and the path of life we are trying to lead, and giving them permission to ask us regularly about our life, what films or TV we have watched, our relationships and so on. The prospect of knowing we might have to own up to someone will often provide the extra restraint that stops us putting a foot on the slippery slope of indulged lust, leading us somewhere we don't want to go. The discipline of fellowship can be a strong help in this area, with people who know us, trust us and can gently keep us (and we can keep them) walking the path we all want to go on.

Lust twists relationships. It messes them up, and destroys beauty and innocence. Christian approaches to sex at first sound restrictive. In fact they liberate us to relate to each other as people, keeping sex in its rightful, wonderful place. Lust is selfish, and as such it is a cruel parody of love. Lust takes; love gives. Just as gluttony is disordered desire for the good gift of food, lust is disordered desire for the good gift of sex. The Christian life is a journey on which our desires are put in balance again and brought back under control so that they enhance rather than wreck our lives and the lives of others. Yet there is one other major area of desire that needs to be ordered rightly: our desire for wealth. That is where we turn next on this road – the deadly sin of greed.

The point is, ladies and gentleman, that greed – for lack of a better word – is good. Greed is right. Greed works. Greed clarifies, cuts through, and captures the essence of the evolutionary spirit. Greed, in all of its forms – greed for life, for money, for love, knowledge – has marked the upward surge of mankind. And greed – you mark my words – will not only save Teldar Paper, but that other malfunctioning corporation called the USA.

These are the words of Gordon Gecko, Michael Douglas' character in the film *Wall Street*, making a classic apology for avarice. Today, greed is good. As Donald Trump once said: 'The point is that you can't be too greedy.'

Gecko's creed is a contemporary version of the highly influential theory stated in *The Wealth of Nations* by Adam Smith, the eighteenth-century philosopher and economist, that self-interest, rather than tending towards the impoverishment of others, actually leads to the benefit of society:

It is not from the benevolence of the butcher, the brewer, or the baker that we expect our dinner, but from their regard to their own interest. We address ourselves, not to their humanity but to their self-love, and never talk to them of our own necessities but of their advantages.

Smith imagines a society in which each person beavers away to provide for their own family and fortune. The outcome is that more goods are produced which, as a result of a mysterious process that he called an 'invisible hand', tend to get shared out, if not equally, at least sufficiently, to all and sundry. He appeals, it seems, not to our altruism but to our greed to make society function properly.

So surely there must be something right with greed? Is it really so bad? Why does it appear on the list of the seven deadly sins when we can see many positives resulting from a little harmless self-interest? Is greed not, as the Scottish philosopher David Hume called it, 'the spur of industry'? Without some element of greed, would not the economy and all human progress grind to a halt? Isn't greed essential to these?

Greed and Self-interest

Before we get too confused, there are some crucial distinctions to be made here between self-interest, ambition and greed. Self-interest, at least in the sense that Adam Smith meant it, is the responsibility to look after ourselves, as well as those who depend on us, and to ensure that we don't abandon our obligations. If we have dependants, we have a responsibility to care for them. We cannot look after them if we have no resources with which to do so. Nor can we do so if we neglect our own basic welfare, health or income. Furthermore, as we'll see later on in this chapter, enjoying the fruits of wealth is by no means a bad thing. Ambition likewise is healthy and vibrant, spurring us on to achieve more; not wasting our lives, but making them count in some way, hopefully towards something good and worthwhile. Greed, however, is different from either self-interest or ambition.

Despite the way he is sometimes represented, Adam Smith doesn't actually argue for unfettered avarice and against benevolence. He just describes what he sees as basic social and economic reality. His point is that not all self-interest works against the good of society. In fact, when he died he left a good deal of his money to charitable causes: Adam Smith was not Gordon Gecko.

Self-interest is different from greed, but it can soon shade into it. Self-interest has limits. And those limits are the interests of others, when pursuing my self-interest starts to impinge upon the interests of other people. If my desire to get rich starts making me steal from my employer by deliberately falsifying my expenses, then self-interest (the desire to have enough resources to enjoy life and provide for my dependants) has turned into greed (the desire to have more, regardless of how that affects anyone else). Greed kicks in when self-interest ignores those limits, becomes unfettered and runs rampant, uncontrolled by any other factor. Avarice takes over when I begin to imagine that my needs are the only ones that matter, and I don't have to balance mine with those of anyone else. When self-interest becomes the ultimate value, as if no-one else exists and the only thing that matters is my own life and prosperity, that's when greed starts to become ugly. As Peter Kreeft says:

Avarice is not desire as such for temporal possessions... but the immoderate desire for them; for it is natural to desire external things as means, *but avarice makes them into ends, into gods. And when a creature is made into a god, it becomes a devil.*

Legitimate self-interest provides for myself and those who depend on me. A healthy ambition achieves great things. Yet greed always consumes. In particular, it consumes the person it takes hold of. It is never satisfied and is always hungry for more. A person who has given in to greed is always unhappy because they never have enough of anything. Whatever they do acquire is always less than what it might be. To get a 50 per cent pay rise leaves a nagging sense of disappointment because it wasn't 60 per cent. Greed is unpleasant and destructive. Gordon Gecko's problem is that he has confused two very different things – self-interest and greed – and shown the healthy benefits of one while ignoring the destructive power of the other.

Yet greed casts a darker shadow than just making us unhappy and unsatisfied. It also threatens to destroy our world. An economy that is driven by consumption and governments who promise ever-increasing prosperity, because no-one dare promise anything less, will inevitably lead to the depletion of the world's resources so that life will become, quite simply, unsustainable. Greed let loose will destroy our planet and its wealth. More than half of the planet's original forests have already been lost and a third of what is left will disappear in the next twenty years if current trends continue. One-third of the world's coral reefs have been either destroyed or seriously damaged. Over the past 550 million years, there have been five major extinctions of species. Who is to say that we might not be next?

Our desire for a richer, more extravagant way of life will keep on eating up the rainforests, the coal deposits and the ozone layer. We have probably already passed the point of no return on global warming with all its potentially disastrous effects on ice floes, sea levels and deserts. The environmental devastation of the past few centuries is a classic example of the effects of greed: a legitimate desire for prosperity, efficiency and technology, pursued without limits or regard for the effect on the planet, has given us what we deserve. This planet is our home, but it threatens to become our grave. It's an open question how long our planet can survive our greed.

The difficulty of course is telling where legitimate self-interest stops and unhealthy greed begins. Does that boundary come when a family has a roof over its head and food on the table? Does it include spare money to spend on fine clothes, not just functional ones? Does it include owning a home, a second home or even a third? Can the boundary between self-interest and greed be defined by a sum of money or a list of possessions, or is it more a state of mind or heart? Are there limits to self-interest, and when exactly does it become greed? When do we know we have had enough? A Christian way of tackling these tough questions starts at the beginning, with darkness brooding over the void.

Good Creation

There is an objection to greed that is sometimes encountered in Christian writing, which runs like this. Greed has as its object physical, tangible goods rather than spiritual ones, and because spiritual realities are superior, wanting physical things should be avoided as much as possible. We should fix our eyes on things above, on spiritual realities rather than earthly ones.

Can this be right? It would be a bit odd if it were. After all, if God did make us, he seems to have made us rather *physical*. He has given us bodies that are made to sustain themselves through food; we are a species that reproduces itself through sex, which requires the use of our bodies; and as if we didn't know, good food and good sex are very enjoyable. According to Christian understandings of creation, God made it that way. Any idea that greed is bad because it is directed at physical things might be Platonic wisdom, but it isn't Christian.

Despite various attempts by Gnostics and such people, who like to be more spiritual than God,

Christians have always said that the fact that the world is physical and material is a good thing. In this sense, Christians are the most materialistic of people; they believe that matter matters.

God likes making things that we can feel, touch and enjoy. In fact he has made a lot of them for that very purpose. One of the writers in the New Testament complains about people who 'forbid people to marry and order them to abstain from certain foods, which God created to be received with thanksgiving by those who believe and who know the truth. For everything God created is good, and nothing is to be rejected if it is received with thanksgiving, because it is consecrated by the word of God and prayer' (1 Timothy 4:5).

He says 'everything' and presumably he means 'everything'. Chocolate, wine, football, roses, lakes, carrots, granite and mangos. Later on in the same letter the writer claims that God 'richly provides us with everything for our enjoyment'. This is really quite remarkable and very different from the way most people think about God. He has created the world for our enjoyment. He wants us to delight in it and we might even say that he is disappointed if we don't. To turn away from every kind of physical pleasure, as if it is more spiritual to confine oneself to more refined other-worldly things, is actually to offend God, just like being invited to a dinner party and refusing to eat the food. I remember, when my children were small, making them a toy farm. I bought some hardboard, painted it green and brown, bought some plastic pigs, cows and sheep, not forgetting a plastic farmer and his wife, and prepared it lovingly for a forthcoming birthday. It really gave me pleasure to see my kids playing with it, and when they eventually moved on to PlayStations and DVDs, and the farm got relegated to the back of a cupboard, I confess to experiencing a small pang of regret.

Now perhaps that is a small glimpse of how God feels about the world and our enjoyment of it. Christian opposition to greed is certainly not a suspicion of the material, nor a suspicion that enjoyment is a bad thing and to be discouraged as much as possible.

Christian faith criticizes greed for two primary reasons: for what it does to a society which is dominated by it, and for what it does to individuals who cultivate it. Thomas Aquinas explains why he thinks greed is a sin:

It is a sin directly against one's neighbour, since one man cannot over-abound in external riches, without another man lacking them... it is a sin against God, just as all mortal sins, inasmuch as man condemns things eternal for the sake of temporal things.

His first point is the one about boundaries. Greed just

wants more for the sake of wanting more, even if that means someone else goes hungry as a result. The second, though it sounds a bit like the idea that spiritual things are more important than physical ones, is not quite that. The argument is that greed for material things is in fact a distortion of a natural enjoyment of physical pleasure, because it pursues these to the exclusion of more spiritual joy. There is a paradox at the heart of Christianity that is vital to grasp if we are to make sense of the Christian approach to life. Although we need physical things, we need more than physical things. As Diogenes Allen writes: 'We are faced every day with the terrible temptation, the powerful pull of two forces: our need and enjoyment of goods that are of this world, and our need for the good that is not. We need *both*. For we cannot live by bread alone; we do not live without it either.' We were made to enjoy things like a succulent cut of beef, fine claret and the ability to run fast, but we were made for more than that as well. We were made for a relationship with our creator and without it, as Augustine said, our hearts will always remain restless and hungry. Greed tries to satisfy the restless soul with things that were never meant to satisfy it, and temporarily at least silences the desire for God that is the clue and pathway to true happiness. So greed not only steals from others, it also steals from ourselves, and in the process it impoverishes both.

Greed and Rest

We find in the earliest parts of the Old Testament the command to the people of God to keep the Sabbath. When the Christian movement started, Christians shifted the day from Saturday to Sunday and removed a lot of the more detailed rules around it, but in general they held onto the wisdom of this basic idea that gave rhythm and structure to life. Once a week, Christians are recommended to take a day to do as little as possible: a day when we can simply focus on God's goodness, our family, friends, and enjoyment, rather than on what we can achieve or earn.

Sabbath is a crucial antidote to greed because it is a regular weekly reminder that the purpose of life is not career, work, money, deals, degrees and all those things we fret over. It is the enjoyment of God and the good things he has given us. The Jewish and Christian idea of Sabbath is much more than a mere 'day off' to recuperate and recover strength for a busy week ahead. It is not that Sabbath helps us prepare for the real business of life, the work we do from Monday to Saturday. It is the other way round. The work we do during the week builds up to the real climax: the day when we enjoy God and his creation, which is what we are really here for.

So one day a week (preferably Sunday, the day of the resurrection), we are to lay down our usual tasks. This is a day when we try not to answer emails or work calls, hold meetings, read reports, plan business trips or do any more shopping than is absolutely necessary. It is a day for walking in the country, sleeping in a bit longer, meeting with Christian friends and strangers for worship, reading books for the fun of it, dreaming dreams and enjoying food. Greed will make it hard for us to do this. The voice of greed inside us will tell us that there is a lot to do, that if we are going to achieve, to get the promotion, to expand our empire, we will need to keep working. But the voice of God tells us something different. That voice tells us to slow down, to be happy just to be, to slowly learn the great art of doing not very much and feeling fine about it. This takes some learning, but when we do learn it, it is one of the best antidotes to greed there is.

Greed and Giving

But what about our money and possessions? Must we give away all we have and become poor? Should we renounce all our possessions? That might be an effective answer, but in fact, in Christian thinking, the counterpart to greed is not poverty but generosity. There are many complex political factors involved in a response to environmental devastation and global warming, but the first step must be in a fundamental change of heart: a shift from greed to generosity. Unless we learn to replace our avarice with a spirit of liberality, there really is little hope for us or for our world.

Wealthy people may or may not be more tempted to greed than others. Yet they do have more resources. In the Bible such people are not told to become poor, but they are told to become generous:

Command those who are rich in this present world not to be arrogant nor to put their hope in wealth, which is so uncertain, but to put their hope in God, who richly provides us with everything for our enjoyment. Command them to do good, to be rich in good deeds, and to be generous and willing to share.

1 TIMOTHY 6:17–18

If we are to learn to avoid greed, which will damage us and our world, we don't necessarily need to start trying to feel guilty about any wealth we may have, but we do need to start learning generosity.

Poverty may sometimes be a good thing. But it is no guarantee of goodness. It is quite possible, perhaps even common, to be poor yet avaricious. Generosity however is a guarantee of goodness. The person who has learnt generosity as a way of life is consumed with the desire to find ways of giving their wealth away. Poverty is no assurance of virtue, but generosity is.

Generosity is such a good antidote to greed because it sets limits on acquisition and introduces a vitally important factor: the needs of other people who might be the recipients of our generosity. Suddenly, my needs and my gratification are not the only or even the most important things on the horizon. The person who has always been gripped by avarice begins to think about someone else for a change.

But that can be hard. If we try giving up something truly precious to us – a car, a suit, a sum of money that would mean an extra weekend's holiday – we find out how difficult it is. I remember a tramp turning up on my doorstep one cold December night, freezing to the bone. He asked for money but his most obvious need was a coat. So I went upstairs and looked in my wardrobe to find something I didn't need any more. I pulled out an old jacket I hadn't worn for several years. Yet as I walked back down the stairs all kinds of thoughts crowded into my mind: special times I had worn that jacket, how it had fitted me really well and how, maybe, I might just wear it again one day. I began to doubt whether I should give it away after all. Forcing myself, I managed to get downstairs, hand over the jacket and close the door, upon which all the thoughts of why I needed the thing evaporated quickly, leaving behind a surreal sense that I had just experienced the temptation of greed – the wish to keep hold of something I didn't need, and that someone else did.

Everything Comes from Above

So how do we learn generosity? The first step is to begin to reflect on how much we have received that was not ours in the first place. It means beginning to reflect on God's generosity to us. Once we realize that everything we have has been given to us, it begins to be a little easier to let go of it.

Imagine a world where the only fruit was apples, or the only colour was blue, or everyone had the same face. It would be a very different world from this one, and the fact that the world is as it is tells us that if it was made by God, then he must like that kind of thing. He makes variety, colour and difference. The further thought that much of the beauty of the world is hidden from human eyes – in the depths of the seas, the wastes of the desert or the howling winds of the mountains – reinforces the same point: that God likes creating physical beauty just for the sake of it, even if no-one ever sees it.

A moment's thought will bring to mind the things we receive as gifts every day. A roof over our head, air to breathe as we wake up, food in the fridge for breakfast, clothes to keep us warm (or cool in the summer), money in our pocket, and some time to sit down and read a book like this. And that's only one day.

Once we begin to see these things as gifts and not as rights, they take on a different meaning. Their origin lies somewhere else. They are not ours because we have some eternal right to them, either because of our own hard work or moral deserving; they are simply gifts to be enjoyed. Moreover, giving is catching. To view everything we have as a gift gets us into the way of giving in return. It creates a flow of possessions, money and goods into our own hands and then on into the hands of others. To remember every day that every breath I breathe, every morsel of food I eat, every sip of water I drink is a pure gift given from the heart of a loving creator God tells me that I live in an amazing world with generosity right at the centre: a world that works through generosity, not greed.

Not Owned but Loaned

Having established that everything is a gift, there is a further radical stage in the Christian path of learning generosity as an antidote to greed. It is to learn the radical teaching of Jesus that, in real terms, we do not own anything at all. It is to learn to give back the gifts we have been given. Jesus spoke to his apprentices in stark terms:

Suppose one of you wants to build a tower. Will he not first sit down and estimate the cost to see if he has enough money to complete it? For if he lays the foundation and is not able to finish it, everyone who sees it will ridicule him, saying, 'This fellow began to build and was not able to finish.'... In the same way, any of you who does not give up everything he has cannot be my disciple.

LUKE 14:25–33

Can he really mean it? I certainly have not given up all possessions and entered a monastery. Does that mean I am not a disciple? I bet you haven't either. Does that mean you cannot be?

Yet this is what Jesus seems to say. He doesn't say 'Be prepared to give up everything when you're asked' (funny how no-one ever seems to ask us to do that), but makes the bold, blunt statement, 'Give up everything.'

Imagine if everyone did just that. Who would own what was left? If most people gave away what they owned and became penniless, then wealth would end up concentrated in the hands of those who had held on to what they had, people who by definition would probably not be the ones we'd choose to be the guardians of all human wealth. Even if we did give up everything, we would still be dependent on others who did own things to drive us around, keep us fed, give us shelter and so on.

So if Jesus' meaning is neither potential nor literal, what does he mean? Perhaps it is this: when we become followers of Jesus we do give up everything. We acknowledge that nothing we possess is really ours, and we give it back to its rightful owner, God. Yet as we have seen, God tends to work through physical things, not in spite of them. One of the primary ways in which he likes to bless us and everyone else is through physical things. So if as a Christian I 'own' anything, it must be simply because God has loaned it back to me for a while; I am really only looking after it for its true owner, to use for a little while for his purposes in the world and to bless other people through it.

Jesus' parable of the tenants who are given sums of money to trade with while their lord goes away is perhaps the best picture the Bible gives of how money or 'possessions' work in God's kingdom. Whatever a Christian has, she only has it on trust. She has been loaned it by her creator to put to use, to trade with. So, as I look around my home at my computer, my books, my house, my DVDs, my kitchen, my garden or my prize collection of football programmes stretching back to 1970, I am to think of them as things loaned to me, things that are not mine to own, possess or grasp. They could be taken from me at any time and I would have no right to complain. And in particular I am to look for ways in which I can use them to build community, to bring people together, to help the poor and to offer welcome and hospitality to those who lack them.

Imagine owning a car which you decide one day in a fit of generosity to pass on to a friend so it is truly his. One day, he is going on holiday and knows you need a car, so he kindly lends it back to you. Driving the car is a strange experience. It feels familiar; it used to be yours. You know the feel of the clutch, the exact pull of the brakes, the hum of the engine. You might start to think that it was yours to do with as you wish. Then you remember it isn't yours at all. It is only borrowed. You treat it differently, not burning the tyres or taking risks in quite the way you would if it were yours to do whatever you pleased with. You know you don't have it for long; you're looking after it for him, so you treat it with care.

That's close to a Christian view of possessions. They are ours for a while to use, to pass on to others and to be treated with care, because they are not really ours at all. They are there to be used, not to be kept. They are loaned, not owned. In general, Christianity doesn't rail against the possession of wealth, but against the hoarding of it. If everything I 'own' is not really mine, but is just held in trust for the God who is its true originator and owner, then I have a responsibility to think carefully how it can best be used for the good of others, the earth God has made and his purposes in the world.

This view of things paradoxically raises their preciousness and also makes them easier to give up. If I reflect on them as God's gift, I am less likely to take them for granted and more likely to retain an amazement that they have been put into my hands for however long they remain there. I am more likely to see them as holy, sacred, special – God's precious possessions loaned to me for a while.

Yet at the same time, if for whatever reason they

are taken away, or I choose to give them away, then that becomes just a little easier, as they were never mine in the first place. And this leads to the most delicious freedom. Most of us know something of the fun that comes from seeing the face of someone we love light up as they open a gift we have carefully chosen and presented. There is a delight and a freedom in that moment, because it gives us an insight into how God feels as he gives us sunsets and snow and mountains and friendship, and watches our faces light up as it dawns on us how good these things are. Learning that kind of generosity leads to a freedom from anxiety about acquiring more and about whether I have more or less than my neighbours; a freedom from the burden of having to stuff my home with more and more possessions. It leads to the liberty and the joy that come from learning to enjoy giving rather than getting, and becoming a little more like God. This brings us near the end of the journey that is the Christian life.

Whenever we look at a wristwatch, we might think of Alberto Santos-Dumont. He was the son of a hugely rich Brazilian coffee baron, who became one of the pioneers of a new form of travel in the early twentieth century: flying through the air. A reasonably sized crowd watched as the 33-year-old took off in a strange contraption – the *quatorze bis* – from a field outside Paris on 23 October 1906, and flew a total of 60 metres at about 10 feet off the ground. This was the first time a machine heavier than air had flown any distance in Europe. Louis Blériot was to be the first to fly across the English Channel, just two years later, but that day all eyes were on Santos-Dumont. He went on to invent the Demoiselle, the first aircraft to be mass-produced in a factory, capable of flying 8 kilometres at a time. Ask any Brazilian, and they will tell you that it was not Orville and Wilbur Wright who deserve the honours for inventing the aeroplane, but Santos-Dumont. While flying, however, he found it very difficult to keep checking his pocket watch with both hands on the controls. He mentioned this to his friend Louis Cartier, who undertook to solve his problem by producing a custom-made watch to be worn around the wrist on a leather strap, which he could look at while in the air. Santos-Dumont wore it on every flight from that moment, and I'd hazard a guess that you are wearing one right now as you read this, all because of this Brazilian aviator.

We might think a man who could claim to have brought into the world both the aeroplane and the wristwatch would have lived a satisfying life. Yet despite this achievement and the huge fame that went with it, Santos-Dumont's life was far from happy. After a crash in one of his Demoiselles in 1910, he gave up flying altogether. He suffered from various illnesses and soon stopped all his work. After his aircraft were involved in several fatal crashes, his sense of melancholy deepened, and when war broke out in 1914, his early hopes that his invention would help in military defence turned to horror at the way in which it was causing death and destruction all around. Deeply saddened by the results of his work, for the last 22 years of his life he stopped working and fell into despair. He finally committed suicide at his home in Brazil on 23 July 1932.

After years of feverish activity, for the last part of his life he seemed to do and achieve nothing. These were years of sluggishness and listless apathy. The kinds of accomplishments many people would die for were no defence against the demon of despair. Santos-Dumont's story takes us straight to the heart of the last on our list of destructive habits: sloth.

What is Sloth?

Sloth is probably the most perplexing of the seven deadly sins, and the one that is hardest to define. Most people would probably think first of laziness when they think of sloth. On the other hand, sloth is often related to the older Latin idea of *accidia*, which is sometimes translated 'spiritual weariness' or 'despair'. But these two definitions indicate the problem we have with sloth. If it is just sheer laziness, it might be considered as a slight moral failing, but most of us would hardly classify a little idleness as one of the great threats to human life. Sleeping in just a little longer in the morning is unlikely to bring Western civilization to its knees. On the other hand, if it is defined as 'despair', that sounds very close to 'depression', and we know that depression is usually an illness that afflicts some people without their choosing. It is not a freely chosen pattern of life, an act of disobedience to God or anyone else. By this understanding, sloth hardly counts as a sin either. Sloth is either too trivial to worry about, or too involuntary to blame.

Clinical depression is an illness that can hit people for no apparent reason and through no fault of their own. The symptoms are similar, but it is important to distinguish depression from sloth. Depression can be caused by genetic factors, a traumatic event or misuse of drugs. Sloth is not depression; it is another form of despair that starts with small things – a shrug of the shoulders, a turning-away from someone in need, a switching-off of something in the heart. Sometimes it can be caused by disillusionment with life, but it begins a pattern of allowing oneself to drift towards a languid 'couldn't be bothered' approach, which in time becomes a habit of life. Once sloth or spiritual weariness gets hold of us, it is hard to shake off, and it can lead to disaster. Sloth is essentially a giving-up on life, and it leads us to finding no pleasure in life, only a dull, steady torpor that expects nothing new, nothing exciting, nothing worth getting out of bed for. Dorothy L. Sayers wrote of sloth: 'It is not merely idleness of mind and laziness of body: it is that whole poisoning of the will which, beginning with indifference and an attitude of "I couldn't care less", extends to the deliberate refusal of joy and culminates in morbid introspection and despair.'

If we want to imagine the opposite of sloth, then Jesus fits the bill. We can never imagine the words 'couldn't be bothered' on his lips. There was a life lived with passion, intensity, laughter, suffering, joy and pain, in which every person who came near seemed to matter. And yet this was not a frantic life, lived without stillness or peace. The Jesus who stops an angry crowd from stoning a prostitute, touches a leper with his own hand, calms a storm with a word and furiously wrecks false worship in the Temple is the exact reflection of the passionate God we might expect from the Old Testament. This God is the complete opposite of grumbling sloth, and such passion is what will develop inside us if we open our lives to him.

Sloth in History

The identification of sloth as one of the chief sins of human life goes back to the lists of sins compiled by the early Christian monks, and it can probably best be understood in that context. John Cassian was one of the founders of Western monasticism, that great movement which kept learning, civilization and scholarship alive in Europe during the Dark Ages. He founded a monastery near Marseilles and some time between AD 425 and 430 he wrote the *Monastic Institutes*, a guide to the monastic life that became one of the standard texts for aspiring monks.

In this book, Cassian outlines 'eight principle faults' of the monks (which incidentally overlap but don't entirely match our list of seven), among which is the 'spirit of *Accidie*'. Imagine a group of monks, all in their desert cells, getting on with their reading, weaving shoes or mattresses from reeds, or saying their prayers. Yet one of them is bored, restless and wishing he was somewhere else. Cassian describes his thoughts:

He often groans because he can do no good while he stays there, and complains and sighs because he can bear no spiritual fruit as long as he is joined to this group; and he complains that he is cut off from spiritual gain, and is of no use in the place, as if he were one who, though he could govern others and be useful to a great number of people, yet was helping no-one, nor profiting any one by his teaching and doctrine. He talks up distant monasteries and those which are a long way off, and describes such places as more profitable and better suited for salvation; and besides this he paints the conversation with the brothers there as sweet and full of spiritual life. On the other hand, he says that everything about him is rough, and not only that there is nothing edifying among the brothers who are around him, but also that even food for the body cannot be procured without great difficulty. Lastly he fancies that he will never be well while he stays in that place, unless he leaves his cell (in which he is sure to die if he stops in it any longer) and takes himself off from thence as quickly as possible.

Although he is referring to the life of a desert monk, what Cassian describes is still a common feeling. Sometimes we think that the circumstances we find ourselves in are hopeless, that nothing can be done about them, and we wish we could somehow run away or escape. As a result everything seems boring; we become listless, lacking in motivation, not seeing the point of anything. We end up just grumbling about everything. It looks like laziness because we don't really want to do anything, but in reality and at a deeper level it is a kind of despair that sees no point in life, and no point in carrying on. That's exactly the kind of feeling Cassian describes in his wayward monk. It's also a very common feeling for many contemporary people.

Cassian's account of *accidia* highlights one key aspect of sloth: it often shows itself in restlessness, a lack of contentment that derives not from envy but from desperation. Envy thinks that if it can only get hold of the thing that is envied, then it will be satisfied. Sloth is beginning to think that satisfaction can never be found. The main thing on the mind of Cassian's fidgety monk is not really the other monasteries that he imagines are so great, but the shortcomings of his own. The reality of course is that they are no more perfect than his own; his imaginings are just fantasy. He is unable to find satisfaction in anything around him and hardly notices the other monks, the opportunities to do useful work, the surrounding landscape. He is always dissatisfied, moaning and finding no pleasure in anything real, only in what is imaginary. It leads to frustration and shoddiness. Wendell Berry describes this as 'the bad work of despair, done poorly out of the failure of hope or vision'.

Sloth and Stimulation

Our culture is the most over-stimulated in history. Only a generation or two ago, children had to make do with a football, a doll, a game or two and a few friends. Then black-and-white computer ping-pong was born, closely followed by Space Invaders, and we all thought the ultimate in entertainment had arrived. We were never to be bored again. Those games now look stone-age. Yet with the arrival of unlimited information at the click of a mouse and games with lifelike graphics, enabling us to fly the world, fight the Second World War and create our own civilization, have we eradicated sloth or boredom? If anything we have increased it. Peter Kreeft comments:

How do we explain the irony that the very society which for the first time has conquered nature by technology and turned the world into a giant fun-and-games factory, a rich kids' playroom, the very society which has the least reason to be bored, is the most bored? Why is the American child playing with ten thousand dollars worth of video equipment more bored than an Indian child playing with two sticks and a stone?

The problem is that however intricate the technology, however scintillating the entertainment, it soon gets superseded by something else. Hence it's hardly surprising that we turn our noses up at the triumphs of yesterday, as we have something better today, and that we even get disillusioned with today's wonders, knowing they will soon be consigned to history as well.

Thomas Aquinas describes sloth as 'sadness and

abhorrence or boredom regarding a spiritual and divine good'. He refers to what happens when, through numerous small choices and turning points, a person becomes incapable of being stimulated by anything good or beautiful or wise; or worse, when goodness, beauty or wisdom evoke a response of disgust or a cynical smirk. When we lose the passion for life, goodness, laughter and joy, then it may be a sign that sloth has fixed its grip on us.

Looking at the other sins, we might be forgiven for thinking that they were a long list of restrictions, a denial of some of the fun things in life, a restriction on our pleasure-seeking, a dampener on passion. It is the inclusion of sloth on the list that gives the lie to this once and for all. Sloth is precisely a lack of passion, a settled laziness that for whatever reason fails to get worked up about poverty or homelessness, AIDS or hunger. It is a dullness that fails to wonder at green rolling hills, brooding mountains, an act of sheer unexpected kindness, the birth of a baby, the work of Botticelli, Mozart or U2 (take your pick from the last three, or add more – beauty is naturally subject to taste). It is the spirit that reacts to cruelty, injustice and pain by shrugging the shoulders and switching the channel. Christianity encourages a passion for life and all that is good and beautiful. That is why it is fundamentally opposed to sloth and puts it firmly on the list of habits to be shunned at all costs.

Christians are intended to be the most passionate of people, but they are meant to be passionate about things that matter, not things that don't. A growing likeness to Jesus Christ means we start getting as angry at suffering and evil as he did, and we develop a similar capacity for life, passion and love.

At the beginning of this book, we saw Julian Baggini's list of seven contemporary sins, which included thoughtlessness ('the intellectual flabbiness of our mentally unfit culture') and complacency ('there's always more we can do and learn, and we should never forget it'). Yet where do these come from? We all know thoughtlessness and complacency when we see them – always more in evidence in other people than in ourselves, of course – yet are they not symptoms of something deeper, a more fundamental malaise of the soul, of which they are only the tip of the iceberg? They are the manifest evidence of sloth. When someone has given up on life, when the most common statement on their lips is 'I couldn't care less', or 'Whatever', when they have become so deadened that no progress seems possible or worthwhile and no wider need beyond their own is recognized – that is when thoughtlessness and complacency rear their heads. We stop thinking about life, ideas or people when we no longer believe that there is anything worth thinking about. Complacency creeps up on us when we assume that there is nothing new to learn, nothing worthwhile to pursue. They both derive from a slothful giving-up on life.

The Origins of Sloth

So where does sloth come from? And how does it grow in a person's life? The Christian answer to that question goes back to our 'createdness'. A surprising witness to this basic insight is the atheist philosopher Friedrich Nietzsche. In a slightly tongue-in-cheek section of his work *The Antichrist* he imagines that God created the world out of boredom:

The old God, wholly 'spirit', wholly the high-priest, wholly perfect, is promenading his garden: he is bored and trying to kill time. Against boredom even gods struggle in vain. What does he do? He creates man – man is entertaining. But then he notices that man is also bored. God's pity for the only form of distress that invades all paradises knows no bounds: so he forthwith creates other animals. God's first mistake: to man these other animals were not entertaining – he sought dominion over them; he did not want to be an 'animal' himself. So God created woman. In the act he brought boredom to an end – and also many other things!

Leaving aside the rest of Nietzsche's rather

tendentious argument in this section, he puts his finger on something quite crucial. Boredom comes from non-existence. When there is nothing there, only boredom is left. God creates the world out of a desire to make something good, something interesting; to stop sloth and boredom. Sloth belongs to non-existence, when everything returns to nothing, when our very existence becomes a burden to us, when we no longer delight in what we see and touch and feel around us. Sloth is an undoing of creation, a denial of the goodness of the world around us.

According to the Christian account of life, we are beings created with a capacity for immense joy, passion, wonder, inquisitiveness and emotion. The world was created as an arena for all this enchantment. It was made so that we might regularly sit back in amazement at the fact that we get to live this life, this physical and spiritual life on this planet that is our home, a place of sheer beauty, encompassing the majesty of a lion, the speed of a hummingbird, the taste of pure water. We were intended to take delight in such things, to explore them and enjoy them; yet most of all we were intended to delight in their creator, the author of all this goodness, the one from whom they (and we) all come, the most beautiful and desirable one of all. In his great autobiographical reflection, entitled *Confessions*, Augustine says to God of the human race, 'They choose to look for happiness not in you, but in what you have created.' Augustine himself was never quite sure whether taking pleasure in created things was a good idea or not. However, he did at least make this one point supremely well: that our ultimate joy is to be found in God. The joy we find in sunsets, friends and apple tart are tasters, anticipations, to give us a taste for the very best, which is God himself. And conversely, when we lose our taste for God, we are likely sooner or later to lose our taste for other good things, or even to develop a taste for things that are bad for us but that imitate the ecstasy of knowing God, such as hallucinogenic drugs or the thrill of theft or cruelty.

Sloth begins with losing our appetite for God. This can happen to religious people just as much as it can to irreligious ones. Many a Christian has learnt to substitute a taste for liturgy, church music or theological ideas for a desire for God himself. As Peter Kreeft puts it: 'There is one thing that never gets boring: God... therefore if we are bored with God we will be bored with everything.' Dante described sloth simply as the 'failure to love God with all one's heart, all one's mind and all one's soul'.

The Remedy for Sloth

So what is the antidote to sloth? First of all, there is one thing to make clear: the opposite of sloth is not workaholism. It doesn't involve the frenetic activity of the aspiring social climber or ambitious careerist. Working sixteen hours a day, seven days a week is not the remedy for sloth; it is the road to a nervous breakdown. As we have seen, sloth is not mere laziness; it is a deeper loss of passion and love for life. The workaholic in fact denies himself the chance to find that wide embrace of life and love and God because he is focused on trifles like a large salary or the admiration of his peers.

How can we restore the delight in life and the passion for goodness that are the opposites of sloth? Thomas Aquinas, writing about sloth, quotes the advice of the book of Ecclesiasticus: 'In order to repel this apathy, the wise man warns: "Bow your shoulders and bear spiritual wisdom, and do not grow weak in its bonds."' His advice is to listen to the spiritual wisdom of people who know better, masters of the spiritual life. Of course one of the effects of sloth is to make us think that no-one has any wisdom to impart, that all advice is pointless and not worth listening to. Yet Thomas's words are wise. If we make ourselves listen for a while, even though it feels like a burden to be borne, we might be surprised.

One of those very spiritual masters or purveyors of spiritual wisdom is the apostle Paul. In one of his letters, he encourages his readers to 'rejoice in the Lord always'; in other words, to find joy in God, to take delight in the best and most enjoyable. Yet this might seem a step too far: a bit too holy, a little too religious to entice. So instead, he outlines a useful way to begin doing this: 'Finally, brothers and sisters, whatever is true, whatever is noble, whatever is right, whatever is pure, whatever is lovely, whatever is admirable – if anything is excellent or praiseworthy – think about such things' (Philippians 4:8). His advice is simple: fill your minds and attention with things of goodness, beauty and health, and slowly you may find this passion for life returning. There is a general principle of life that if we put trash in, we can expect to get trash out. Filling our minds with stuff that is shallow, flashy and glittering but lacking in substance quickly leads to boredom. Bad films, pornography, voyeuristic reality TV and superficial people never satisfy for long. They are the mental and spiritual equivalent of a cheap hamburger: it looks and tastes good, but soon leaves a stale taste in the mouth and a definite hint of indigestion.

Instead, advises Paul, try to find things that have real depth and value. These might include really good books, paintings, TV programmes, conversations or walks in the fields. When we do this we find that several things begin to happen. We begin to lose that self-centred discontentment with life and are reminded that there are things worth getting out of bed for; there are things in the world that can inspire and energize us. We find ourselves lifted out of the torpid drudgery of a life that has lost its passion, and we are redirected towards things that can pull us in the right direction. We also find that as we fill our minds and hearts with goodness, the anomaly of evil becomes more and more stark. When we encounter people who are systematically denied the basic needs of life – food, water, work, dignity – we begin to be stirred by it, even angered. When we see the environment scarred by pollution or deadened by decaying, drab concrete ugliness, we are more likely to be struck by the contrast with the beauty of real nature, and to begin to feel that this should not be.

The next stage comes in the next thing Paul says: 'Whatever you have learned or received or heard from me, or seen in me – put it into practice. And the God of peace will be with you.' In other words, just do something. John Cassian directs his impatient monk to some other words of Paul and describes the effect of the apostle's words:

The cause of all these ulcers, which spring from the root of idleness, he heals like some well-skilled physician by a single salutary charge to work; as he knows that all the other bad symptoms, which spring as it were from the same clump, will at once disappear when the cause of the chief malady has been removed.

The contemplation of good things can only take us so far as a remedy for sloth. If that is all that we do, we soon return to indolence, idleness and the same old round of boredom. It needs to be followed by action, commitment to some worthwhile cause, to making a difference in the world. It doesn't matter a great deal whether it is action for the promotion of something positive, such as creating music, writing down ideas or building friendships with neighbours, or the eradication of something evil, such as poverty, lack of education or homelessness. The key thing is that we do *something*, commit ourselves to *something*, out of a vision of what it might achieve, and break out of the idleness that Cassian diagnoses as the root of the disease of spiritual apathy.

The final step is joy – when we are able to 'rejoice in the Lord'. This is the true Christian antidote to sloth. If the Christian analysis is that underneath all despair and boredom is a loss of appetite for God, then the deepest answer to it is to rediscover that appetite, that simple enjoyment of God. This can seem a long way off, but for some of us God is an acquired taste. I remember my first taste of Guinness. The dark, swirling Irish drink had always had a fascination for me when I was growing up, and I remember the first time I plucked up the courage to look older than my age and bought a can in the local store to give it a try. It was foul. I hated it – it tasted sour, bitter and unpleasant. It didn't help that it was a hot summer's day and the beer was warm, but that didn't matter. It was the kind of experience that might have made me never touch the stuff again. It wasn't until later on that, a few years older and after a bit of perseverance, I began to appreciate the hidden flavours, the rich, full, wheaty taste. I realized that just because it didn't taste like lemonade this did not necessarily mean that it was bad. As I learnt to appreciate and enjoy it, Guinness soon became a favourite drink, something I would choose above all others.

If it doesn't sound too irreverent, for many people it is a bit like that with God. The idea of enjoying God may be about as appealing as that sip of Guinness was for me aged sixteen. Yet in time, we can learn to appreciate things that have a deeper richness, a more profound taste. Guinness is obviously a trivial example, but the same can be true of God. An acquired taste can take a while to come, but when it comes, it is the richest of all.

We perhaps have a mental image of a contemplative, someone who finds their deepest joy in God, as other-worldly, not much use for getting things done. Yet when we look closer, it doesn't work that way. Some of the people who have achieved most in the field of goodness and love have done so out of a deep joy in God. A lady called Miss Sullivan wrote a letter to a friend in 1815 in which she described William Wilberforce, the man who did most to bring to an end the dreadful blight of slavery in the British empire: 'By the tones of his voice and expression of his countenance he showed that joy was the prevailing feature of his own mind, joy springing from entireness of trust in the Saviour's merits and from love to God and man... His joy was quite penetrating.' Setting aside the somewhat quaint language, she hits upon the secret of Wilberforce's achievement: he was able to enjoy God.

There is an apparent paradox that only those who have made some progress in the spiritual life know: that the closer we come to God, the more we love what is good and want to see it spread, and the more we detest evil and want to see it finished. When we meet a Christian who doesn't respond this way it's likely they have never quite grasped the heart of Christianity, or if they did, they have lost the fascination for God that they once had. Although when we first think of it sloth might seem the most trivial of sins, in fact it may be one of the worst, because it brings despair and darkness, denies the goodness of what God has created and results in a sullen indolence. The opposite of love is not hatred, it is indifference. If indifference is at the heart of sloth, then sloth is the enemy of love, which makes it the enemy of the best thing there is: the heart of God, the life that lies at the centre of the world.

Yet there is a way out of sloth, just as there is always a way out of all sinful habits. It lies in learning to worship and enjoy God, giving thanks for God's forgiveness, grace and goodness not just in church (though of course it includes that) but also as a daily habit of life, recognizing God's hand in every good thing we see, every kind act, thoughtful gesture or thing of beauty. It involves the commitment to fruitful action and the discovery of joy. We are beckoned to start walking that path, the path that leads away from destructive habits and builds a truly good life, a path that starts with God and ends with God.

Our journey is over. Starting with the challenge to step down from our pretentious claims to rule our own little worlds, our journey has shown us how to accept forgiveness and the person God has made us to be, to hand over control to God and to order our desires rightly for food, sex and money. Sloth may seem an odd place to end, but it is vital because overcoming sloth leads to true passion: a fuller enjoyment of and engagement with life than we ever thought possible. Sloth is overcome when we learn again what the human race had at the beginning: a simple, uncomplicated enjoyment in the presence and love of God our creator. Although this is the end of this particular journey, in a sense the journey never ends with God. As we learn to enjoy God again, there is no end to that particular pleasure, no final resting point. It is instead an endless voyage of delight that not even death can bring to an end.

Sin	Spiritual disciplines	Virtues	Spiritual steps
Pride	Confession and service	Humility	Repentance
Envy	Faith	Contentment	Faith
Anger	Silence	Peace	Forgiveness
Gluttony	Fasting	Temperance	Self-control
Lust	Fellowship	Love	Respect for others
Greed	Sabbath	Generosity	Liberality
Sloth	Worship	Passion	Desiring God

Aelred of Rievaulx, *Spiritual Friendship* (translated by Mary Eugenia Laker), Kalamazoo, Cistercian Publications, 1977.

Allen, D., *Spiritual Theology: The Theology of Yesterday for Spiritual Help Today*, Cambridge, Mass.: Cowley, 1997.

Allen, D., *Temptation*, New York: Church Publishing, 2004.

Aquinas, T., *On Evil* (translated by Richard Regan, edited by Brian Davies), Oxford: Oxford University Press, 2003.

Augustine, *Confessions* (translated by Henry Chadwick), Oxford: Oxford University Press, 1998.

Charry, E., *By the Renewing of Your Minds: The Pastoral Function of Christian Doctrine*, New York: Oxford University Press, 1997.

Dante, *The Divine Comedy* (3 vols), Harmondsworth: Penguin, 1955.

Delumeau, J. and E. Nicholson, *Sin and Fear: the Emergence of a Western Guilt Culture 13th–18th centuries*, New York: St Martin's Press, 1991.

de Botton, A., *Status Anxiety*, London: Hamish Hamilton, 2004.

Facaros, D. and M. Pauls, *The Travellers' Guide to Hell*, London: Cadogan Guides, 1998.

Fairlie, H., *The Seven Deadly Sins Today*, Notre Dame, Indiana: University of Notre Dame Press, 1979.

Hauerwas, S., *Vision and Virtue: Essays in Christian Ethical Reflection*, Notre Dame, Indiana: University of Notre Dame Press, 1981.

Hauerwas, S. and C. Pinches, *Christians Among the Virtues: Theological Conversations with Ancient and Modern Ethics*, Notre Dame, Indiana: University of Notre Dame Press, 1997.

Kreeft, P., *Back to Virtue*, San Francisco: Ignatius Press, 1992.

Lewis, C. S., *Mere Christianity*, London: Fount, 1997.

Meilaender, G., *The Theory and Practice of Virtue*, Notre Dame, Indiana: University of Notre Dame Press, 1984.

Pieper, J., *The Four Cardinal Virtues*, Notre Dame, Indiana: University of Notre Dame Press, 1990.

Plantinga, C., *Not the Way It's Supposed to Be: A Breviary of Sin*, Grand Rapids: Eerdmans, 1995.

Schimmel, S., *The Seven Deadly Sins: Jewish, Christian and Classical Reflections on Human Psychology*, New York: Oxford University Press, 1997.

Sennett, R., *The Corrosion of Character: The Personal Consequences of Work in the New Capitalism*, New York: Norton, 1998.

Tomlin, G., *Spiritual Fitness: Christian Character in a Consumer Culture*, London: Continuum, 2006.

Wilkinson, H., *Beyond Chaotic Eating*, Petworth: Roper Penberthy, 2001.

Willard, D., *The Spirit of the Disciplines: Understanding How God Changes Lives*, London: Hodder & Stoughton, 1988.

Willard, D., *Renovation of the Heart: Putting on the Character of Christ*, Colorado Springs: NavPress, 2002.

Willimon, W. H., *Sinning like a Christian: A New Look at the Seven Deadly Sins*, Nashville, Abingdon Press, 2005.

For those interested in finding out more about Christian faith from the beginning: www.alpha.org

Also available from Lion:

UNSEEN FOOTPRINTS

Sheridan Voysey

Do you ever wonder about the unseen reality that lies beneath the surface of your world? Have you ever glimpsed something unexpected that seems to take you out of your normal routine for a few moments? A splash of colour that offers the extraordinary in a world of otherwise routine monotony? Perhaps it's a meaningful interaction with a friend, a precious conversation with a sibling, a beautiful landscape viewed or a moment of self-awareness so heightened that something bigger than your mere individual existence is touched upon. At such times, the veil is lifted and you glimpse the possibility of another, more vibrant, world.

Unseen Footprints offers a journey in search of this other world, the world of the divine. Drawing on his own faith journey and featuring evocative quotes, stories and photography from contemporary life, the author coaxes the reader into the complex search for meaning and purpose.

ISBN 978-0-7459-5293-2

SEARCHING 4 FAITH

Brian Draper

How do we find faith today in our materialistic culture? Is it possible to believe in Christ? Brian Draper approaches the subject in an imaginative, poetic way, drawing on images from contemporary culture to help present the case for Christianity.

Divided into three sections entitled The Way, The Truth and The Life, the author discusses questions such as: Who was Jesus? What path should I choose? What do I have to do to get some peace round here? Must I go to church to be a Christian? How do I make the most of my life?

Part of Lion's *Questions of faith* series and illustrated throughout with colour photography, this contemporary and innovative book is an ideal introduction to the key issues of coming to faith for those seeking God both inside and outside the church.

ISBN 978-0-7459-5195-9

All Lion Books are available from your local bookshop, or can be ordered via our website or from Marston Book Services. For a free catalogue, showing the complete list of titles available, please contact:

Customer Services
Marston Book Services
PO Box 269
Abingdon
Oxon
OX14 4YN

Tel: 01235 465500
Fax: 01235 465555

Our website can be found at:
www.lionhudson.com